Haunted Herefordshire

Haunted Herefordshire

by

Rupert Matthews

Logaston Press

LOGASTON PRESS
Little Logaston Woonton Almeley
Herefordshire HR3 6QH
logastonpress.co.uk

First published by Logaston Press 2008
Copyright © Rupert Matthews 2008

ISBN 978 1904396 98 7

Typeset by Logaston Press
and printed in Great Britain by
Bell & Bain Ltd., Glasgow

Front cover: Avenbury church

Contents

Acknowledgements

All the photographs have been supplied by myself, with the exception of those of Croft Castle on p.11 and Goodrich Castle on p.37 for which acknowledgement is due to John Wilson.

Introduction

Herefordshire is one of the most beautiful counties in England. The Golden Valley is famous for its scenic beauty, but the wider Wye Valley has its fans, while the Lugg to the north has a charm all its own. There are hills, valleys and forests enough to satisfy anyone interested in natural beauty.

Nor are the towns and villages far behind in attraction. Hereford is perhaps the most charming of English cathedral cities — certainly it is one of the smallest and most rural. The Cathedral seems timeless, though it is not the first to stand on this site. Ledbury, Leominster and Kington are just three of the charming towns that dot the county.

But Herefordshire is not all peace and tranquility. In the past this has been a wartorn region as English and Welsh fought for control of the richer acres of the county, or Cavalier and Roundhead squabbled over who should rule the kingdom. These violent events, and many others, have left their spectral mark on Herefordshire. It is difficult to think of a county that can boast more ghosts, or a wider variety of spooks, spectres and phantoms of all kinds. Some of these otherworldly visitors are gentle, some mischievous and a few downright evil. Some haunt ruined castles or churchyards, just as ghosts should in the popular imagination. Others pop up in village streets or in welcoming pubs. The phantoms of Herefordshire are nothing if not varied.

In putting this book together I have travelled all over the county searching out spooks, legends and strange stories. I would like to thank Pete Kensell and Tim Brown who came with me on legs of my journey. Above all I must thank the people of Herefordshire, who have been so welcoming to me and so willing to share their supernatural heritage.

1 Ghosts with a Purpose

In ghost stories and horror movies, ghosts are generally a fairly unpleasant bunch. They are not only capable of appearing from nowhere, and then vanishing just as abruptly, but they come to the world of humans on missions of unremitting evil. Even those that are not intrinsically wicked tend to be ill disposed to humans. Whatever the purpose that lies behind the haunting, it bodes no good.

Fortunately such phantoms are very rare in reality. The vast majority of ghosts are rather ambivalent toward the living. When they notice us at all they rarely do anything to interfere with the world of humans, preferring to fade away back whence they came.

One very obvious exception is the dark phantom of Aconbury. This spectre seems to have come straight out of the worst kind of horror movie. For a start it haunts a site that is spooky in the extreme. The little church of St John the Baptist is one of those sad rural churches that stands half neglected amid waist-high grass and brambles that run riot in the church-yard. The crumbling walls and overgrown graves make this an atmospheric place to visit. It is quite easy to imagine a ghost here.

If the locals are to be believed, however, imagination is not needed. The ghost that haunts this churchyard is tall, dark and malevolent. He dates back to the days when this was not just a busy church, but the centre of a priory of nuns of the Austin Order. The priory was founded in the early 13th century and by the time it was closed down during Henry VIII's dissolution of the monasteries, it was a noted school for the education of young ladies.

As a renowned centre of learning the priory attracted wealthy benefac-tors. One such was Sir Roger de Clifford. This knight was an offspring of the famous Clifford family that came to England with William the Conqueror and by so doing acquired wide estates and much wealth. He spent little time at home, being often away in command of the king's troops.

As his time to die approached, Sir Roger entered into an arrangement with the godly nuns of Aconbury that was not at all unusual for the time.

He gave them a substantial sum of money in return for being buried in the priory church. Part of the deal was that the nuns would mention Sir Roger regularly in their prayers. It was confidently believed at the time that such prayers would mitigate the sins of the person for whom they were said and reduce their time in Purgatory, or even in Hell.

We may not believe such things these days, but Sir Roger did and it is this that has led to the haunting. When the priory was closed in 1536 the nuns were ejected to live off a modest pension. The buildings were demolished and the materials sold off to fill King Henry's coffers, while the little church became the parish church of Aconbury.

The new parishioners, reflecting the changed theology of the Protestant era, did not continue to pray for the soul of Sir Roger Clifford. His sins were now believed to be a matter between him and God in which other humans could not interfere. His tomb remained, however, and soon the trouble began.

The ghost of Sir Roger began to be seen near his tomb inside the church. He was clearly unhappy that the prayers for his soul, for which he had parted with good hard cash, were no longer being said. After a century or so the

The overgrown porch to the little church at Aconbury. The ghost here is one of the most terrifying in Herefordshire

ghost had increased his activities to the point where he would wander around the church and churchyard disrupting services and scaring the hapless parishioners.

The then vicar consulted his neighbouring clergy and decided to conduct an exorcism. The rites of exorcism were then less formalised but more common than they are today. The vicar knelt beside the haunted tomb, deep in prayer, with a candle, a Bible and a bell. The ghost duly arrived and tried to blow out the candle. If the ghost had succeeded, the exorcism would have been defeated. But it was the vicar who won, by the devout fervour of his prayers. As was the way then, the unquiet

spirit of Sir Roger was confined to an everyday object — in this case an old bottle, which was firmly corked as soon as the ghost was forced inside. The bottle was then bricked up in the church wall just below the tomb.

The parishioners of Aconbury must have thought that they had finally seen the last of Sir Roger. But some time in Victorian days he was back. Presumably the bottle had cracked open, perhaps as the walls of the church had settled. Whatever the reason, the ghost was back and more vengeful than ever after his enforced stay in the musty old bottle.

The tall, dark ghost of Sir Roger now stalks the semi-abandoned church and its churchyard. If you see him, you had best make yourself scarce. So angry is this ghost that he seeks to reach out with his skeletal arm to touch humans on the shoulder. And if he should succeed, his very touch is death. Those few who have been touched have all died within a year.

On the few occasions when the old church is unlocked it is possible to view the fateful tomb of Sir Roger Clifford. It must be admitted that not many people take up the opportunity.

A wooden carving in the porch at Aconbury dates back to the time this was a medieval priory the time when the haunting began

Rather more successful was the exorcism of the ghost of Garnstone. This phantom took the unusual form of a gigantic white calf that wandered the area at night. The ghost was widely held to be that of a farmer who had committed suicide just before the spectral calf was first seen. The vicar decided not to give the ghost time to announce its purpose, but imprisoned it in a snuff box, snapped the lid shut and threw it into the village pond. There it remains, and the ghost with it. Unsurprisingly the villagers have never felt the urge to dredge the pond.

No such mystery surrounds the reason why the wicked ghost of Penyard Castle lurks around the old ruined walls. Buried deep beneath the ground in two wooden barrels is a vast store of gold. The barrels lie in a cave, the entrance to which is barred by a pair of iron gates which stand at the end of a long tunnel. The entrance to the tunnel is hard to find, and the route itself is partially fallen in. This might be just as well.

Back in the early 19th century a local farmer decided to try his luck at getting the treasure. He knew that the gold was guarded by a spirit set there by the last owner of Penyard Castle, but thought he knew how to defeat it. Yew wood had the reputation for being proof against witches, while rowan (known locally as quicken) was said to deter the little people. The farmer therefore made a harness out of yew for his pair of plough oxen and a goad of rowan for himself.

He then clambered down into the tunnel and tied a rope from the harness to the iron gates. Using the goad he got his oxen to start pulling. With much effort the team jerked the gates open. In excitement the farmer saw the rumoured barrels beyond the doors, overflowing with gold coins.

'Ha', called the farmer in excitement. 'I believe I shall have it.'

Suddenly the rope broke and the gates slammed shut. A phantom jackdaw then appeared and regarded the farmer with a malevolent eye.

> Had it not been
> for your quicken tree goad
> And your yew tree pin
> You and your cattle
> Had all been drawn in

crowed the bird before disappearing in a flutter of wings.

The ruined gatehouse of Longtown Castle. Once a key fortress on the English – Welsh border, it now lies in ruins and is the haunt of a most unusual phantom

Also guarding a treasure is the ghostly bird of Longtown Castle. This time the hoard takes the form of a thousand golden guineas buried in a wooden coffin. Nobody has yet managed to find the coffin, let alone retrieve the gold coins. The ghostly guardian is doing its job well.

Such ghostly treasure guardians are a speciality of Herefordshire rarely found elsewhere, another example of which exists at Bronsil Castle, just outside Eastnor. This time the phantom takes the form of a gigantic black raven which haunts the island at the centre of the moat. This raven is possessed of the supernatural ability to confuse visitors, causing them to wander blindly past the pit that holds the vast treasure of the Beauchamps, who used to live here. The raven is waiting for the rightful heir to the Beauchamp estates to visit and only then will it reveal the hoard.

Another treasure once lay at a farmhouse near Bromyard, but its ghostly guardians have long since gone. The haunting began in the 1820s when a new tenant came from outside the area to the farm after two old spinsters had died leaving nobody to take over. It took the form of a clattering and banging that shook the house almost every night.

Unsurprisingly, servants and workers soon refused to stay at the farm overnight, preferring to slip back to their own homes at dusk and return at dawn. This did not suit the farmer, who wanted somebody to get up early to light the kitchen fire and cook his breakfast. The farmer's desire for a servant, and the reason for it, spread far and wide.

Finally a young slip of a girl from Hereford city presented herself at the door and offered to take up the position. 'I'm not afraid of the Devil himself', she declared to anyone who queried her decision. It was not long before her boast was put to the test.

One evening as she dozed in her kitchen chair, the girl was awoken by the usual clattering and crashing. Boldly she glanced around the empty kitchen. 'I'm not afraid of you', the girl declared. 'In the name of God, who are you?'

At once the noises stopped, to be replaced by an unnerving silence. Then a small glow appeared in the corner of the room, followed by a second. The glows grew and gradually took on the form of two elderly ladies dressed in long silk gowns. The ladies walked towards the cellar door, then turned to beckon the Hereford girl to follow them. Boldly, she did so.

The ghostly ladies led her down to the dank cellar and silently pointed to a particular flagstone in the floor. Grabbing a handy pickaxe, the girl set to work to lift the stone. After some struggling she got it up and saw an old casserole dish hidden beneath it. Glancing at her ghostly companions, the girl bent down and lifted the lid off the dish. It was filled to overflowing with gold coins.

The ladies let out an audible sigh. They explained that they had buried their treasure there when they were alive, but had been unable to retrieve it before their deaths. The hidden gold had kept them chained to the farm, stopping them from moving on to the next world. Now that the gold had been found, they were free to pass over. They advised the girl to split the gold with the farmer, then vanished.

The girl did as the ghosts had directed her and then slipped off back to Hereford with her share of the booty. Neither she nor the ghosts troubled Bromyard again.

It was not hidden gold but hidden documents that led to the haunting of Black Hill Farm, near Craswall. This ghost took the form of a pale face that peered in through the window at the inhabitants. The farmer and his family were too frightened to challenge the ghost, and so the haunting continued.

At the local hiring fair one spring the farmer hired a farmhand who came from some distance away and knew nothing of the ghostly face. He was alone in the kitchen one night when the face appeared. Startled, the new man called out 'Who are you? What do you want?'

Finding its voice at last, the ghost replied simply 'Come away'. The labourer was seized by an overwhelming urge to follow the ghost that he could not resist. The ghost led the hapless man over the hills for what seemed like miles until it came to a stone wall and pointed to a particular stone. The man pulled the stone out to reveal a box. 'Fetch it', ordered the ghost.

The man extricated the box, and was then powerless to stop himself from following the ghost again. Once more the pair set off over the hills and down until they reached a stream. 'Empty it', the phantom ordered. The man opened the box, pulled out several bundles of what looked like old legal documents and hurled them into the stream.

'It is done', the ghost declared. 'I will trouble neither you nor others again.' With that the ghost faded from sight, leaving the startled man all alone on the banks of the stream as dawn was breaking. Not knowing where he was, he wandered off down the valley and eventually came to a hamlet. He was by this time in a sorry state, suffering from the cold and with one foot badly cut, as he had lost a boot somewhere on his travels. He never recovered from his encounter and suffered from what modern doctors would probably call shock or post traumatic stress disorder. His must have been a severe case, for he did not survive long but fell sick and died. The ghost, however, was gone for good.

Another bundle of old documents brought distress to one Tom Ackley of Kinnersley in the 1840s. Every day at dawn Tom would walk from his home to Weobley to begin work, then at dusk he would walk back. One day as he walked through the fields he saw a lady dressed in white watching him from a distance. He thought this odd and told his family about it.

Next day the lady was there again, and the next and the next. Each day she watched Tom from a slightly different place and each time she was closer to him. Finally she came so close that Tom could see her face clearly and realised that she was nobody local. After a fortnight of this, Tom was walking home when he met the lady sitting on a stile and blocking his route. It was only then that he realised that the lady was a ghost. The two looked at each other in silence for some time. Then Tom summoned up his courage and asked 'Please, lady, let me pass on my way home.'

The ghost smiled and replied 'I have been waiting for years for somebody to speak to me. I am Lady Berrington and am trapped here on Earth. Now follow me and do my bidding so that I may be released.' She got down from the stile and led the way over the fields to the grand farm of Devereux Wootton.

The ghost walked up to the front door, which at once flew wide open. Hesitantly, Tom followed the ghostly lady into the house. It was now almost dark and he saw that the servants had left their shoes in the kitchen, indicating that they had gone to bed. Nobody awoke as the ghost led Tom up to the attic. With a wave of her arm, she caused an old wooden chest to be revealed, then bent forward, opened the chest and extracted a bundle of old parchments.

The ghostly Lady Berrington gave the documents to Tom telling him to take them to the nearby pond and throw them in. 'If you hear sweet music', the ghost explained, 'I will have gone to my rest. But if you hear cursing, I will have gone to the Other Place.'

Tom hurried down the stairs and ran to the pond. He threw the documents in and for a few fleeting seconds there came the most beautiful singing that he had ever heard. Then he collapsed and was found unconscious by the pond next morning. Like the unfortunate labourer of Black Hill Farm, Tom never really recovered. He was ever after a bit slow and simple, though his life was not cut short.

If the ghosts of Black Hill Farm and Devereux Wootton treated their human companions harshly, the ill treatment was the other way round at Acton Cross in the 1830s. Mrs Hodges, the wife of the village blacksmith, died leaving her husband with two small children. Mr Hodges married again, with what the villagers considered rather indecent haste, to a woman from a neighbouring village.

The new Mrs Hodges had no time for the children of her predecessor and treated them badly. Soon after the wedding, the ghost of the first Mrs

Hodges began to appear. At first she would stand beside the beds of her children at night and smile at them. Soon, however, she began to roam about her old home. She usually appeared alongside her children as if to protect them from their stepmother.

As might be expected, the new Mrs Hodges did not care for the phantom intruder, so she went to see the local vicar, Reverend William Copeland, who was new to the parish. It seems she spun him some story, for he agreed to carry out an exorcism. Coming to the forge with a Bible and candle in the approved fashion, Copeland raised up the ghost, then overcame her by the power of prayer and confined her in a matchbox. He then threw the matchbox into a pond. It seems a harsh fate for a mother whose only aim was to protect her children.

The purpose of the ghost that lurks upstairs at the Falcon Hotel in Bromyard is very clear, but sadly nobody can help him. The ghost was first seen in 1964. He appeared to be a perfectly normal young man dressed in the fashions of the time. It seems that the first few people to see him did not realise he was a phantom, so solid and normal did he seem to be. It was only when he was seen several times, appearing and disappearing from nowhere, that it was realised that a haunting was going on.

The ghost walks yet. He paces down the corridor calling out 'Where is Anne?' Who he was, and who Anne might be, nobody knows.

Also harshly treated by the humans he met was the ghost of Mr Hoskins, one of the staff at Hereford Cathedral. This Mr Hoskins did not go as

The Falcon Hotel in Bromyard is haunted by a ghost that was first seen in 1964

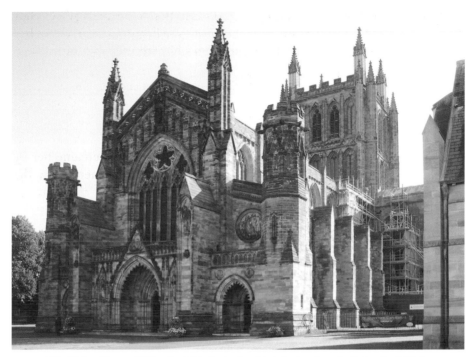

The West Front of Hereford Cathedral, which had to be rebuilt in the 1780s, apparently as a direct result of the haunting of the nave by a Mr Hoskins

tamely as did Mrs Hodges. After his death in 1786 he was seen pottering about the Cathedral as if continuing with his duties. This might be thought a fairly harmless occupation for a ghost, but the clergy decided to lay the ghost nonetheless.

Twelve of the cathedral clergy gathered in the nave one night, each armed with a Bible, a Prayer Book and a candle. At 11pm they formed a circle and sat in absolute silence until midnight. Then, as the great bell tolled, they lit their candles and began to pray. The ghost did not come at first, but eventually turned up looking very angry and distraught. 'Why so fierce?' enquired one clergyman. 'Fierce as a man, much more now a devil!' the spectre replied. He began to blow out the candles of the clergy, one by one until the only one left alight was that held by elderly Canon Underwood. There were some tense minutes while the canon prayed and the ghost stormed about. Then the ghost crumpled. Underwood took his chance and sent the ghost to be trapped beneath the bridge at Byster's Gate.

As he went, the ghost of old Hoskins raised a terrible commotion banging on the walls, rattling the doors and filling the cathedral with unholy screeching. Two days later the West Front collapsed.

The hills and fields around Longtown are haunted by the friendly phantom of Thomas Hutton

Altogether more friendly is the ghost of Longtown. This phantom is that of Thomas Hutton, a shepherd who lived in the village and died in about 1875. He spent most of his life out on the Black Mountains looking after his sheep, frequently staying out in the isolated stone huts that dot the hills, or even sleeping in the open on fine nights. After his death he was often seen striding over the hills, and he frequently pointed travellers in the right direction.

The story told by a man who met the ghostly shepherd in 1895 is typical. 'I had been to see friends at Llanthony and was returning directly over the mountain when a fog came on suddenly and I lost my way. I was standing, quite bewildered, when a man came towards me wearing a large, broad-brimmed hat and a cloak. He did not speak, but beckoned, and I followed him until I found myself on the right path. I turned to thank my unknown friend, but got no reply. He walked off quickly into the fog. This seemed strange, but I thought no more of it.' It was not until the man was visiting Longtown a few days later and told his story that he heard the tale of the ghostly shepherd in the wide-brimmed hat and realised that his silent saviour had been a phantom.

Since motor cars became commonplace, the phantom shepherd has not been seen much. It is to be hoped that he has not yet given up his mission

Croft Castle is haunted by the benign spectre of Sir James Croft who built the structure and remains intensely proud of it long after his death

of guiding people over the mountains, for the fog can come down quickly to catch out hikers and walkers.

Another benign phantom is that of Sir James Croft of Croft Castle. He rebuilt the northern side of the castle and clearly loved the estate. His ghost is seen only when building work is going on. Then he will appear for a few seconds as if inspecting the changes being made to his old home before gently fading away. Presumably he returns to ensure that the work is to his liking.

Considerably more violent was the ghost of the Rhydspence Inn just outside Whitney-on-Wye. Today there is a toll bridge over the river beside the village, but before the first bridge was built (in 1779) there was a ferry which charged a penny for each crossing. On busy days the ferryman did a roaring trade and amassed a great number of pennies, which he kept in a metal pot tucked in his boat. At dusk he went home, carrying the pot with him, and locked it in his kitchen.

One evening a pair of evil characters used the ferry while travelling away from Hay. They spotted the pot bulging with coins and decided to have it for themselves, so they lay in wait for the ferryman and pounced as he walked home. The poor man was killed in the struggle that followed, and the two thieves ran off. They got as far as the Rhydspence Inn and then decided to stop there for the night.

Having taken a room, the pair came down to the bar to drink and eat, using their stolen money. Eventually they went to bed, but some hours later the entire household was awoken by a terrible commotion coming from the room occupied by the two murderers. The landlord burst into the room to see the two men cowering in the corner while the pot of money danced a little jig by itself on the floor. The pot stopped as soon as the landlord came

Whitney's Rhydspence Inn was the venue for the ghost of a vengeful man that made sure that the men who had murdered him did not escape justice

in, but it had done its work. The landlord recognised it as that belonging to the ferryman and guessed that the two men had stolen it. He locked them up and sent for the local magistrate. Next day the body of the ferryman was found.

The two men later confessed to their crime. Apparently the ghost of their victim had come to them at the Rhydspence Inn. It had been the ghost that had been pushing the pot about, although the landlord had not seen it. The two murderers were hanged in Hereford for their crimes.

Another murder that came to light through supernatural means took place on the Black Mountain sometime around 1840. One of the shepherds running his sheep on the hills was a noted local wizard who was rumoured to have the power to talk to animals. Whether that were true or not, he was a prosperous old man who did not suffer fools gladly. He managed to earn the enmity of two brothers from Longtown, also shepherds on the Black Mountain.

One unfortunate day the brothers came across the old man all alone in a secluded spot. They drew their knives and closed in. The old man looked up calmly, realising that he had no way to escape. He uttered a strange croak and a crow came fluttering down. The old wizard glared at the brothers. 'If you kill me', he said, 'the very crows will cry out and speak of it.' The brothers laughed, killed the old man and stole his money before going on to steal most of his sheep. The crow flew off.

The Black Mountains seen from Longtown. Sometime around 1840 a murder was committed high on the slopes that led to a haunting in the village

A few days later the brothers returned to Longtown. As they entered the village a flock of crows came down to whirl around their heads calling loudly. Whenever the brothers stopped, the crows would come down to sit about and watch them. When the brothers moved the birds would take wing and circle above them calling.

Such bizarre behaviour could hardly be missed and soon the villagers began to wonder what the birds were up to. One man decided to follow the brothers to try to find out. He crept after them as they walked out of the village and hid in a hedge to eavesdrop as the men talked. 'Brother, do you recall how when we killed the old shepherd up on the mountain there,' said one brother, 'he said that the crows would cry out against us?'

It was enough for the men to be arrested. Their home was searched and several items belonging to the murdered man were found. They were, of course, hanged.

Also intent on righting wrongs, though she has proved to be less successful, is the ghost of Lady Sarah Tempest who haunts the lanes around Colwall. Lady Sarah was born plain Sarah Lambert to Mr and Mrs Lambert of Hope End House. Her mother died when she was still a teenager. Mrs Lambert left her considerable fortune, including the house and estates, to her daughter instead of to her husband.

In 1790, this fact came to the ears of Sir Henry Tempest, a handsome, dashing and utterly penniless baronet from Yorkshire. He came down to

Herefordshire determined to marry the heiress. Tempest began his campaign by staying away from Colwall itself, but questioned anyone he could find who had been there. He learned that Sarah was a plain girl much given to superstition.

Sir Henry disguised himself as a gypsy fortune teller and made his way to Colwall. He managed to accost Sarah and offered to tell her fortune. The girl agreed, and Sir Henry told her that if she went to Colwall church next day at a certain time she would see the man that she would marry sitting in the porch.

Superstitious as she was, Sarah duly went to the church, perhaps expecting to see some local man. She was overcome with pleasure to find, instead of a dull Herefordshire farmer, a dashing gentleman with a title. Tempest brought his considerable good looks and charm to bear on the young girl and in less than a fortnight she had agreed to marry him. Mr Lambert opposed the match, but Tempest had prepared for that. On 24 January 1791 he whisked Sarah off on a romantic elopement to be married in a distant parish where the vicar was not too fussy about the proprieties of such matters.

The church at Colwall is but one site in the village where the ghost of Lady Sarah Tempest returns in an attempt to right wrongs

Returning to Colwall, Tempest took possession of Hope End House, evicting his father-in-law, who went to live at nearby Barton Court. A few months later, Tempest and Sarah had a blazing row. Tempest threw her out and, since her father would not see her, the hapless girl went to live with an elderly relative some miles away.

Poor Sarah died soon after and it was not long before her ghost began to be seen flitting about Colwall. The ghost was persistent and seen often, weeping and wailing. Tempest was not a man to put up with such revenge from beyond the grave. He sold up and left. Hope End House was bought by a Mr Barrett, whose daughter Elizabeth wrote of the ghost 'I have heard that now she has not merely a local habitation but a name for she is said and devoutly believed to be Lady Tempest who was the proprietress of this house before Papa bought it. I hope that she may keep the bridge and not show any other local attachments.'

Ironically Elizabeth Barrett would herself elope with a dashing young suitor against her father's wishes. Fortunately Elizabeth's marriage to the poet Robert Browning proved to be a happy one.

These days the ghost of Lady Tempest still walks the lanes around Colwall, being seen most often near Hope Hill House, a private residence not open to the public. Those who have seen her, describe the ghost as being that of a young woman in a long dark gown who emits a feeling of great sadness. As well she might.

The purpose of the ghost that appeared in Ledbury on 1 December 1950 was clear enough; the ghost came to announce his own human death. The apparition in question was that of the composer Jack Moeran, who lived in Ledbury with his mother. When inspiration was short he would walk around the town and countryside deep in thought. If anyone tried to talk to him while he was thus engaged he would hold up his hand and move off.

In November 1950 he left to visit friends in Ireland, saying that he would not be back until Christmas, so when a woman he knew saw him walking down Ledbury High Street on 1 December she assumed that he must have come back early for some reason. She crossed the road to talk to him, but Moeran held up his hand in the familiar gesture, indicating that he wished to be left alone. The woman turned aside and walked on. It was not until some days later that she heard that Moeran had died suddenly in Ireland at about the time that she had seen his apparition.

The ghosts of Pencombe came with a definite purpose in mind and, having achieved it, have not been seen recently. The old church, built around 1200, stood some distance away from the village beside a lane. By the mid 19th century this church was in a state of grave disrepair and a decision had to be made as to whether to repair it or pull it down and build a new one.

Given its poor state and inconvenient location, the parishioners decided to pull down the church and build a new one in the centre of the village. This they did and the beautiful style church that was completed in 1865 makes a visit to the village even more worthwhile. The spirits of those who had been buried at the old church, however, did not seem to have appreciated the move. They began to be seen moving around the old churchyard, then came out to walk up the lane to the new church, all the time wailing and sobbing.

A hurried meeting was held. It was decided that the old churchyard should continue to be treated as consecrated ground and to receive burials. That seems to have satisfied the unquiet dead, and explains why the churchyard of Pencombe is some distance outside the village while the church stands in its centre.

2   Phantom Monks and Ghostly Clergy

There is something irresistible about ghostly clergy. Every part of Britain has its tales of phantom monks, spectral nuns and unearthly vicars. Herefordshire is awash with them. It can sometimes seem as if almost every village has its ghostly monk or nun flitting about.

Quite why this should be is not entirely clear. Being devoted to the sacred things of life, the clergy have no obvious reason to be more prone to returning as ghosts than anyone else. If, as some believe, ghosts are the wandering spirits of the uneasy dead, then the clergy should not really feature at all.

Others believe that ghosts are more like recordings of dramatic events that are somehow held in the walls of houses or the stones of the landscape. These recordings are imprinted by the strong emotions of those involved in events and can be replayed back if the conditions are right. The recording then appears as a ghost. Again, clergy are not noted for their tempestuous lives so why they should imprint their emotions on the landscape more often than others is not clear.

One ghostly friar whose story has survived for centuries was the anchorite of West Hide Wood, near Tillington. Exactly when this rather worldly cleric lived is unknown, but given that his job was to tend the small shrine that lay in the woods it must have been before the Reformation.

Whenever he lived, the friar was fond of slipping away from his religious duties to participate in the gambling and drinking that went on in Tillington. One day the friar had completed his morning devotions and settled down to lunch when a passerby told him that a badger baiting was due to take place that afternoon and invited him to come along. The friar refused, knowing that he had more prayers to say for the souls of the departed that particular day.

But then, what should come snuffling into his little chapel but a badger? The friar could not pass up such a chance. He hurriedly grabbed a sack and bundled the badger into it. Then, forgetting his duties, the friar slung the badger over his back and hurried off toward Tillington.

The Bell Inn has traditionally claimed to have been the venue for the badger baiting, and for what happened next. As the friar walked along he thought he heard a voice coming from the sack, but discounted this in his haste to get to the Bell. He trotted up to the pub and the crowd of drinkers gathered outside, calling out that he had a fine, strong badger in his bag. He then put the bag down and opened it. Out sprang the devil himself, shouting 'Daddy calls'. He grabbed the friar and both of them disappeared in a ball of flame before the startled eyes of the drinkers. To this day a ghostly monk may be seen hurrying toward the Bell Inn at Tillington. The rotund figure scurries along as if in a great hurry. He stops just outside the inn, and then vanishes into thin air. The locals have a saying, 'Where the Devil got the friar', which means that something has been achieved by trickery or deceit, for the Devil got the friar by tricking him into abandoning his religious duties.

Another monk has often been seen at St Peter's Church in Hereford. This figure is tall and wears a long cloak that reaches to the floor and rises up to form a hood that hides the phantom's face. The ghost is seen most often in December. In 1926 a pair of policeman spotted a hooded figure walking up to the door of the church, and then vanishing into thin air. Thinking that the figure was some miscreant hiding from them, the policemen searched the area thoroughly and only then accepted that they had seen the ghost.

St Peter's Church in Hereford is the haunt of a phantom monk
that appears around Christmas time

There are two stories to explain this ghostly figure. The first is that he was a monk cut down at the altar of the church by marauding Welshmen on one of their periodic raids into England. Alternatively he is thought to be the ghost of Sir Walter de Lacy. It was de Lacy who built the church for the use of the monks in the 1080s. It is thought that de Lacy intended to become a monk when he reached old age, but didn't live long enough. One December he was visiting St Peter's to confer with the abbot when he met with a tragic accident. The two men had gone up the tower so that the abbot could point out some features of the city to de Lacy, when the knight slipped on a patch of ice and fell to his death. It is said that the ghost is the shade of de Lacy returning to walk about the church in death as the monk that he never became in life.

On balance the story about de Lacy is probably to be preferred, if for no other reason than that the story of a monk killed by the Welsh is repeated in rather more detail in connection with a ghostly monk at the cathedral.

This monk is seen most often near or in the Lady Chapel. He is dressed all in white and is said to date back to the fateful year of 1055. The previous year two events happened some distance away that proved of great importance to Hereford. First, Gruffydd ap Llywelyn, Prince of Gwynedd and Powys managed to impose his rule on the petty princes of southern Wales, uniting Wales after a fashion. Second, Earl Aelfgar of Mercia was angered by King Edward the Confessor for taking Mercian territory to create the earldom of Hereford. Over the winter Aelfgar travelled to Wales by way of Ireland to meet with Gruffydd. Together the two men hatched a plot to bring down Edward and set up another ruler in his place — perhaps Aelfgar.

As the good weather of spring arrived, Gruffydd and Aelfgar struck. The combined armies of the Welsh princes poured over the border near Hay-on-Wye and streamed down the Wye valley. The local English ffyrd, or militia, were called out to muster at Hereford and messages sent east to King Edward. Aelfgar also sent riders east to rouse his supporters in the hope of sparking an uprising against Edward.

The Herefordshire ffyrd met the invading Welsh somewhere near Kenchester. Although the precise site of the battle has been lost, its result is clear. The English were crushed. Refugees streamed back from the battlefield to Hereford. The city was hurriedly abandoned and a long wagon train of refugees headed for the better defences of Worcester. The only men left in Hereford were the canons and monks who served at the cathedral.

When the Welsh arrived, they found the city deserted. Looting began and soon several houses were going up in flames. When the raiders reached the cathedral close they were met by the seven canons who explained that the cathedral and its buildings belonged to God, not to the King of England. There was a tense stand-off for a while as the numbers of Welshmen, many of them by now drunk, increased.

Suddenly one Welshman drew his sword and hacked down one of the canons. It was enough to start a general slaughter of the canons and monks. One monk raced to pray at the high altar of the cathedral. As he heard the Welsh approaching the monk grabbed the jewelled cross, turned and held it high over his head. It was no good; he was hacked down like the rest.

A few weeks later the main English army arrived under the command of Earl Harold Godwinson, later to be the King Harold killed at the Battle of Hastings. Two years of warfare followed, ending in a compromise peace by which Aelfgar was restored to his titles and lands and Gruffydd was given estates in Cheshire, though he had to accept that Edward was his superior and his lord.

It is the monk who was slaughtered at the high altar who is generally thought to be the tall figure in white that lurks around the Lady Chapel. The old English cathedral has long since been demolished and replaced by the present structure. So far as can be deduced, the old high altar lay close to the present Lady Chapel.

He is not the only phantom monk in the city, for Westfaling Street also has its cowled monkish ghost. No dramatic story attaches to this haunting. The ghostly monk simply appears, walks down the street for a few seconds and then vanishes again.

Similarly enigmatic are the two ghostly monks of Craswall Priory. They have been seen frequently pacing gently among the ruins. Presumably they are the wraiths of some medieval holy men who lived out their lives here and return in spectral form to enjoy the peaceful solitude of the quiet ruins.

The Talbot Hotel at Leominster has a ghost that is generally thought to be that of a monk. He certainly looks like one, appearing dressed in a long grey cloak complete with a cowl and hood. That there was a monastery here is well known. The monk William of Winchester was living here in 1281 when he wrote the song *Sumer is icumen in*, one of the earliest surviving songs written in English. He was later excommunicated for unspecified but easily imagined acts involving women that breached his monastic oaths. Nobody has ever been able to prove that the Talbot Hotel or its site ever had anything to do with the monastery, so it is not entirely clear why a monk should haunt the place.

The ghostly monk of St Weonard's Church is similarly out of place, for the church has never had any known link to a monastery. Perhaps the ghost is that of a former clergyman who favoured monkish robes over those more usual for a vicar.

Another religious phantom haunts the lanes near the charming church of St Dubricius at Hentland. She is a lady in a grey cloak, usually described as being a nun. There was a small chapel here in medieval times run by the nuns of Aconbury Priory, but there does not seem to be any other evidence that the phantom lady is a nun.

She is, however, remarkably active and has been seen many times. In 1953 a local man was cycling down one of the many lanes thereabouts that are lined by high hedges and banks. As he came racing round a corner he was confronted by a lady in the middle of the road. He slammed on his brakes and juddered to a halt, but the woman had gone. Given the high, steep banks there was nowhere she could have scrambled so quickly, so she must have been the ghost.

It is not only monks and nuns who return in spectral form. Quite ordinary vicars are seen as phantoms as well. One such stalks the road leading into Peterchurch from Hay. The vicar walks with stately and measured tread while staring straight ahead and looking neither to left nor to right. Behind him comes a horsedrawn hearse carrying a coffin. The small procession moves in absolute and eerie silence.

The story of a rather peculiar phantom vicar was told to the Reverend Thomas Lewis in around 1895 by a dying parishioner as a deathbed confession. The man said that when he was a young man his house had been plagued by a ghostly vicar. This phantom was dressed in a long black cloak and had a tightly curled white wig, a costume that would put the original human being firmly back in the 18th century.

The church of St Dubricius at Hentland is home to a ghostly monk

The ghost spoke to the man in Welsh, asking him if he would go to Clifford Castle to perform an errand. The task was to extract some money from a hiding place and then throw it into the river. Following the instruction, the man found the money — a few coins of silver — and threw it into water. The ghost was then seen no more.

The dying man was clearly greatly troubled by these events and wanted to know if he had committed a sin by conversing with a ghost. The Reverend Lewis set his mind at rest.

Hellens House at Much Marcle is unique in having not one but two phantom clergy. The first and the less active is a nun who walks down the stairs from time to time. The second is the ghost of a priest who was killed here during the Civil War of the 1640s.

Herefordshire was overwhelmingly Royalist. Hereford declared for the king when hostilities began, and the area was a rich recruiting ground for the king's armies. Despite this the area saw little in the way of serious fighting. It was too far from the main strategic goals of the two sides, so apart from some desultory raids mounted by the Parliamentarian forces in Bristol not much happened in the county.

Not much, that is, until the summer of 1645. By that date the war was as good as over. The king's armies had been comprehensively defeated at the battles of Marston Moor and Naseby. All that Parliament needed to do was sweep up the few recalcitrant fortresses still held in the king's name and impose its will on areas, such as Herefordshire, that did not recognise its right to rule.

So it was that an army of Scots led by Lord Leven came to Herefordshire. They failed to take Hereford city itself, but swept through the countryside looting the property of anyone who opposed them and burning several houses. When they got to Much Marcle the Scots found a sullen population willing, albeit grudgingly, to accept the rule of Parliament. But the parish priest would have none of it. The king was, he said, the lord's anointed. The Scots dragged him to Hellens House and subjected him to a severe beating in an effort to change his mind. They failed, but the man's injuries were so severe that he later died. The room where the deed was done is still haunted by the unhappy spirit of the poor man.

Rather happier, though no less determined, is the ghostly vicar of Kinsham. There are various different versions of the story of the bell of Kinsham, but all agree that many years ago the good folk of Kinsham decided that they wanted to have the best and finest bells in the county of Hereford. They collected a great sum of money, then sent an order off to a bell foundry abroad for a fine set of bells. The bells were cast and shipped

Figure of a saint in a niche at Kinsham Church

to Bristol, where they were loaded on to a barge to go up the Wye and then the Lugg to Kinsham.

The trouble began when the bells arrived at Kinsham. The first few were unloaded easily enough, but when the largest — nicknamed Tom — was being moved the ropes broke and it fell into the river where it was seized by an evil spirit. It is here that the various versions of the story diverge.

According to some versions, the villagers try all sorts of ploys to get the bell out of the river, but always fail for one reason or another. Another version has the villagers fail, but then tells of a passing clergyman who wades into the river praying as hard as he can while a team of oxen strain on the ropes tied to the bell. Eventually the vicar's determination wins out and the bell is hauled onto the riverbank. The vicar himself, however, is never seen again. It is this man's ghost who is seen pacing between the church and the River Lugg.

The church bell at Aymestry was similarly linked to evil spirits, though here it is the bell itself that is said to have the power to defeat them. The bell was until fairly recent times rung at sunset. The reason usually given for this was that the sound of the sacred bell was enough to keep the little people tied to the nearby Pokehouse Wood, a place of evil reputation. In fact it seems more likely that the bell was a curfew bell that continued to be rung long after most curfews ended. In any case the little people have not been reported to have been seen recently, bell or no bell.

A very different sort of phantom lurks among the deeply atmospheric Avenbury Church ruins. These tumbled walls stand at the end of an overgrown drive closed in by tall trees that cast their gloom over the scene. Around the church stands a crumbling stone wall and dozens of gravestones and tombs — some intact, others leaning at crazy angles, and all disappearing into a mass of brambles, ivy and undergrowth. There are few weirder places in all England. From these tumbled walls there will sometimes drift the sound of peaceful organ music, though there has been no organ here since the church was abandoned almost a century ago.

The phantom music is the result of a brutal crime perpetrated some time around the year 1800. There were at that time two brothers living in Avenbury. One was an industrious and hard-working farmer who was popular with his neighbours and noted for his fair dealing in business matters. The other was what Herefordshire folk call a sclem, a lazy wastrel. The first brother used to play the organ in the church during services, practising alone of an evening.

One day the two brothers fell out when the first refused to pay off yet another gambling debt incurred by the second. The sclem brother nursed his grievance, convinced that his brother was wealthy merely because he was lucky rather than because he worked hard. As the ne'er-do-well wandered alone and bitter he heard organ music start up and knew his brother was in the church. He decided to lie in wait and take by force the money that he could not get by pleading. The plan was put into effect, but the fight turned savage and the good brother was killed by the bad one. The murderer fled and was never brought to justice.

Perhaps because of this the ghost of the victim comes back to Avenbury from time to time to play his beloved organ, sending music wafting gently out over the ruined church.

There was another ghostly phenomenon at Avenbury. It was said that the church bell would ring of its own accord whenever the vicar of Avenbury lay dying. When the church was closed down, the bell was moved to St Andrews-by-the-Wardrobe in the City of London, which was in need of one. The parish of Avenbury is now no more, having been merged with that of Bromyard. Amazingly the bell has been heard to ring on its own even in its new home. It last did so in the 1990s, though the vicar of Bromyard and Avenbury was in perfectly good health at the time.

Perhaps the answer to the riddle of why there are so many phantom clergy about lies in the clothing that they wear and people's imaginations. A good many ghosts, spectres and apparitions are seen only for a second or two and often in poor light. They may be glimpsed rather than seen and perceived only as a vaguely human outline of a greyish colour. Searching through history for a figure that matches such a vague description, a monk or nun makes an obvious candidate.

This is not to say that all ghostly monks are cases of mistaken identity. Where there is a definite story attached to the ghost, or where it appears in the ruins of a monastery, the ghost could properly be taken to be that of a monk or nun. But ghost hunters have come to be wary of ghostly clergy. They very often turn out to be something else, or nothing at all.

3 White Ladies

If there is one type of ghost that is quintessentially English, it is the white lady, and Herefordshire seems to have more of these enigmatic spectres that most counties. Perhaps there is something about the gentle hills and attractive villages that draws these ladies — and they are always ladies, never women.

Take for instance the white lady of Middleton. She is a quiet, gentle soul who likes to drift around Gravenor's Bridge just outside the village. Who she might be and why she feels such an attraction to the bridge is unknown, but there must be some reason why she keeps returning. The white lady who haunts the lanes near Court Farm outside Snodhill is similarly anonymous and enigmatic, as is the white lady of Eardisland.

Snodhill has a second white lady, who haunts the old manor house and its grounds, but she at least has a purpose. The manor house was built in 1660 by the Prossers, who continued to live there until 1878. This lady is thought to foretell a death in the Prosser family, or at least this was so when the Prossers lived there. Whether or not her doom-laden purpose still holds true is unclear. In any case she seems to be linked to a torchlit funeral procession that passes down the lane outside the old manor house from time to time.

Also visiting the mortal world to announce a death is the white lady of Hampton Bishop. She foretells the death not of a member of a particular family but a member of the family of the person who sees her. Sometimes the death she indicates is that of the witness himself or herself. She is a dangerous phantom.

This white lady is generally thought to be that of Isobel Chandos, daughter of the governor of Hereford Castle in the early 14th century. Those were turbulent years for England. In 1307 England gained a new king in the form of Edward II. The new king was weak, indecisive and unpopular. His favourite was a gay young blade named Piers Gaveston, whose witty jests were usually cruel jibes at the noblemen who controlled much of England's lands. In 1312 those noblemen rose up against Edward's inept rule, and made it a condition of any deal that Gaveston had to be banished abroad.

Among those who rose in rebellion was Humphrey de Bohun, Earl of Hereford. He was supported by numerous troops from the county, and the governor of the castle, John Chandos. The rebellion of de Bohun hurt Edward, especially as the earl was married to the king's sister Elizabeth — but then Elizabeth was particularly opposed to Gaveston.

The rebellion ended in victory for the nobles, and they then took matters into their own hands. Given the hated Gaveston as a captive, they did not take the young man to a port to sail into exile. Humphrey de Bohun was among those who took him to a bleak hillside and watched while two Welshmen in the force led by Chandos stabbed him to death, then hacked off his head.

Edward never forgave the men who killed his lover. It took him ten years to regain control of the kingdom and muster his forces, but eventually he was ready. At the Battle of Boroughbridge Edward's men defeated those of the rebel lords. The Earl of Hereford was killed in the fighting.

Chandos was not present at the battle, but Edward had neither forgiven nor forgotten his role in the killing of Gaveston. A party of royal knights was sent riding to Hereford with orders to kill Chandos and any who opposed them. They came to the city and were admitted on showing the king's seal. The unfortunate Chandos was loaded into a boat on the Wye and taken out of the city to be hanged from some convenient tree.

History does not record where he died, but the ghost can tell us. Isobel went with her father on his last journey, and her ghost seems to recreate this terrible ordeal. Standing in a boat she comes drifting down the Wye from Hereford to a meadow just outside Hampton Bishop. The boat comes to shore and the white lady climbs out to stand on the bank. She watches intently as something invisible to those who see her takes place nearby. Then she falls to her knees and breaks out in the most heart-rending sobs and wails. The ghost then reboards the boat and disappears back toward Hereford.

A terrible ordeal for the poor girl. But her own fate was none too pleasant. As the daughter of an executed criminal she became a ward of the king. Edward was a notoriously spiteful man. While the ultimate fate of Isobel Chandos is unknown, it is likely that she was married off to one of Edward's supporters who helped himself to her lands and wealth while giving her nothing in return.

There is an interesting twist to the story, though there is no real evidence for what is in truth merely a bit of local folklore. The story goes that young Isobel was an exceptionally pretty girl who had caught the eye of a young local knight named Sir Hugh Despenser. This Despenser rode off to court to seek his fortune and by the time of the Battle of Boroughbridge was in the king's army. Being from Herefordshire he was one of the knights sent to kill Chandos.

Arriving in Hereford, Despenser tried to save Chandos in order to win the heart and hand of the woman he loved. His subterfuge came to nothing. Despenser found himself hated by Isobel for his role in her father's death and distrusted by the king for his attempts to countermand the execution order. He was subsequently killed by King Edward II for his betrayal.

There was, in fact, a Sir Hugh Despenser the Younger who owned lands in Herefordshire at this time. He was not, however, a native of the county and so far as we know was content merely to collect the rents and delegate the work to a manager. Moreover, he was very much a favourite of King Edward. When Edward's misrule finally became too much for England it was discovered that Despenser had been helping himself to government funds on a large scale. Roger Mortimer, the future Earl of March, and Edward's queen, Isabella, seized control of England in 1326 and sought to take into captivity the king and his main supporters, including Despenser. Despenser fled west and was captured at Neath, subsequently being taken to Hereford where he was beheaded.

It seems that local talk has linked the two dramatic incidents, weaving a romantic tale around what was in reality a pair of rather brutal and sordid events.

Another white lady with an unhappy story is the ghost that lurks on the upstairs floors of Hellens House in Much Marcle. This is the phantom of Hetty Walwyn, a daughter of that famous family of Herefordshire gentry. Young Hetty fell desperately in love with the son of a local farmer who worked as a stablehand at Hellens House. Her love was returned, but her father was predictably outraged by the romance. He forbade young Hetty ever to see the boy again and sacked him on the spot.

A few days later Hetty vanished, as did her boyfriend. The Walwyns sent out riders in all directions to try to catch the eloping couple, but no trace of them could be found. The weeks passed and became months, then years.

Then Hetty suddenly returned home some five years after she had left in such dramatic fashion. On her finger was a stunningly impressive diamond ring, but she had nothing else to her name. It turned out that the couple had gone abroad where the young farmboy had prospered as a merchant, buying his beloved young wife the diamond ring. But tragedy struck when the man fell sick and died. Hetty had tried to keep the business going, but had failed and had spent all her remaining money getting home to Much Marcle.

Her father took her in, but insisted that she had to stay within the house and never go out in case she met some other undesirable young man. Poor Hetty died a short time later, traditionally of a broken heart. She walks around the house to this day in a long hooded dressing gown.

The ghostly white lady of Pembridge has a similarly unhappy tale to tell, but with a happier ending. This spirit is that of Mrs Breton, wife to the vicar of the parish in the 1650s. She had inherited a fair amount of land in her own right and had always intended that one particular field should be left to the parish so that its rent would pay for an annual grant to the local poor. When she died, however, no will could be found so all her lands and money went to her brother. This brother seems to have been a heartless type for he ignored his sister's wishes, even though they were fairly common knowledge.

A few days after Mrs Breton's funeral her ghost began to be seen, pacing back and forth over the field that she had intended to leave to the parish. The story of the ghost spread quickly, but the brother ignored it. Perhaps he thought it an invention of the local poor trying to get him to part with his land. Then the ghost appeared to her old servant. This servant ran home and was so clearly shocked by what she had seen that her new master, the errant brother, believed her tale and handed over the land for the benefit of the poor.

Although the tale has a happy ending, it does not seem to have satisfied the ghost for she is said to walk still.

Another white lady who came to right wrongs is of rather more enigmatic origins. Back in the 18th century a farmer named Higgins worked his land around Little Birch. In one field was a spring, the water of which was particularly pure and sweet. The villagers loved the water and often went to collect it. Higgins, however, grew increasingly annoyed by the constant tramping over his lands, and by the way the villagers kept forgetting to close his gates securely.

In a fit of anger he blocked the spring with stones, earth and other debris. Soon afterwards a phantom white lady began to be seen hovering around the well. Rumours began to circulate that the spring had a ghostly guardian. Higgins ignored the talk. Then one evening as he sat smoking a pipe in front of his fire, water began to well up through the flagstones. Within seconds the kitchen was awash. Splashing through the waters, Higgins retreated outside, to see the phantom white lady watching him from a distance.

The next day Higgins unblocked the spring, then laid a pipe from it to a nearby lane so that the villagers could collect their water without trampling over his lands. The white lady has been seen a few times beside the new wellhead.

The story is interesting for many reasons, not the least of which is the fact that the white lady has not been identified, but appeared only when the spring was blocked. In pre-Christian times many springs, streams or rivers were believed to have their own local goddess who cared for them, and occasionally these deities demanded some form of sacrifice from those who used the water. It may be that the story of Higgins and the well is a garbled version of an old pagan rite or legend that was changed when Christianity arrived. Certainly there does not seem to be any mention in the recorded past of a man named Higgins owning the land where the spring lies.

Some similar origin might lie behind the notorious black lady of the Black Mountains. She is said to be an evil spirit who lures walkers into bogs or close to dangerous drops. She has not been reliably seen for some years, which is probably just as well.

No such mystery surrounds the white lady who walks through Hereford city centre, from the Cathedral west front down to the river. The name of the little street along which she walks gives a clue to her identity; it is named Gwynn Street, and the lady in question is Hereford's most famous daughter, Nell Gwynn.

Nell, or Eleanor to give her the name that she was baptised with, was born in about 1650 in a small cottage that stood in this street. The site of her birthplace is marked by a plaque. While still a teenager the impoverished but very pretty Nell moved to London where she earned a living selling oranges to theatregoers before she became an actress herself. She was an accomplished comedienne and within a few months was the most popular — and best paid — actress in London.

Gwynn Street in Hereford is haunted by the famous lady who gave the lane its name

Nell soon caught the eye of King Charles II, but the first date they had went horribly wrong. Charles invited Nell to dine with him after her show one night, along with his brother the Duke of York and the Earl of Derby. The meal was taken in a tavern near the theatre and the four ran up quite a bill by ordering roasted meats and fine wines. When it was time to pay the bill, the landlord presented the total to King Charles. Charles, however, had come out without any cash so he passed it to York, who was also without any money and turned to Derby, who likewise did not have enough on him to settle up.

'God's Mercy', cried Nell loudly, so that all in the tavern could hear her. 'If I had known you were a parcel of beggars, I should never had consented to dine with you.' And she paid the bill herself before flouncing out. Charles was captivated and before long Nell was his mistress. She bore him two sons and persuaded him to found the Chelsea Hospital for old soldiers.

So far as is known Nell did not return to her old home once she had found fame and fortune in London. Maybe that is why she comes home in spirit form.

A great many white ladies are more or less anonymous. The charming and welcoming Rhydspence Inn outside Whitney-on-Wye has a ghostly white lady. She is said to be a former landlady who was also a witch. There is a white lady who walks the streets of Hoarwithy while another — or it might be the same phantom — is seen down by the bridge over the river. For some reason this particular white lady is said to be a schoolteacher from Victorian times, though there is no particular story attached to her. What appears to be a quite different grey lady frequents the lane outside the village leading to Tressech Farm. The white lady of Kentchurch is similarly anonymous. She is seen looking out of a window of Kentchurch Hall, but is only ever seen by those outside, never by anyone inside the house.

Some ghost hunters are inclined to treat white ladies with a degree of caution, particularly those that cannot be readily linked to a particular person. It is undeniably true that a good many white lady phantoms are said to be seen close to springs or streams, in places where cold water runs on the surface. Such places are prone to patches of mist and some feel that the white ladies reported at these spots are no more than a swirl of mist rising up in a vertical column the size and shape of a woman.

Maybe so, but not all the white ladies appear in such places. Even if they do then, as old farmer Higgins of Little Birch discovered, it pays to treat them with respect.

4 Spectral Transport

It must be said that the internal combustion engine — for all the benefits that it has brought to man — has not been kind to the supernatural world, especially in Herefordshire. Many of the more haunted places in the county lie off the beaten track, often on hillsides or beside streams that can be reached only by footpath or bridleway. In years long gone by the countryfolk used these paths on a daily basis to get to or from work, visit friends or go courting. Now they are trodden only by people out for a quiet weekend stroll, or by ghost hunters curious to locate an elusive phantom. People prefer to drive or travel by bus these days. So there are many ghosts that are rarely reported simply because there are no longer people around to see them.

Nor are cars, buses and lorries prone to become spectral entities after they have been taken to the scrapyard. Perhaps they are simply too mechanical to have a spirit that can return to haunt the world of the living after they have passed on.

But it was not always so.

South-west of the village of Dilwyn stands a grand old house named The Homme. The story goes that one of the servants died in the downstairs area early in the 19th century. The death was officially put down as being due to a sudden seizure, but rumour and gossip abounded that foul play had been involved.

Soon after the death a servant was in the hallway when he thought he heard a coach and horses draw up on the gravelled drive in front of the house. Thinking that some visitor was calling, the servant opened the door but the driveway was empty. A few days later another servant had the same experience — this time she was even certain that she heard a coaching whip crack as the vehicle came to a halt, but again there was nothing visible outside the door.

No actual ghost was ever seen outside The Homme, but the phantom coach continued to be heard every few weeks through the years that followed. Nobody was entirely certain what the link between the ghostly coach and the

31

mysterious death might have been, but the fact that the phantom began to be heard so soon after the death caused everyone to assume that some link existed. Perhaps, some speculated, the coach was a phantom hearse come to collect the dead. But since nobody ever saw the apparition this could not be known for certain.

All that can be said with any certainty is that the ghost was never encountered again.

An equally invisible coach haunts Cut Throat Lane just outside the village of Lea. This particular phantom is rather choosy about when it manifests itself. It is heard only on chill winter mornings as the sun peeps up over the horizon to reveal a thick frost on the ground and decorating the trees. It is said that the phantom coach is heard to move majestically toward the village as if its occupants were off to pay some early morning call — perhaps on one of the ghosts that lurks within the welcoming walls of the Crown Inn at the village centre.

The rather precise nature of this phantom has led some ghost hunters to wonder if it should be consigned to the ranks of those invisible ghosts that turn out to be anything but; more than one supposedly invisible phantom has been found to have a perfectly natural explanation. One well-known haunting in a town house in Bath, for instance, took the form of a piano that was heard to play from a particular room, but only if that room was empty and the door was shut. Close investigation revealed that a piano teacher lived next door. The solid old walls blocked out the sound of the piano, but when the door was shut the room acted as a sounding box and transmitted the music. Once the secret was known, the 'ghost' could be made to perform at will.

Some have speculated that the warming rays of the rising sun striking Cut Throat Lane served to heat up some feature that had been chilled to below freezing by the frost. Perhaps air rushing from a cavity caused a noise similar to that of a passing coach, or maybe defrosting twigs rattled out the sound. Or perhaps, of course, there really is a ghostly carriage that trundles by only on sunny, but bitterly cold winter mornings. Who are we humans to speculate about why ghosts behave as they do?

Another old coach is said to haunt Chance's Pitch, near Ledbury. It is reported that back in 1852 a stagecoach, having left Gloucester at midnight, was crossing the Frome Bridge when it was precipitated into the swollen river, the bridge having been washed away, and a passenger was killed. The ghostly coach that is seen racing past pulled by four horses is certainly of the type used by the companies that ran regular routes between the major towns and cities of England.

An equally ancient form of transport is seen passing underneath the old bridge at Ross-on-Wye. This is a rowing boat of a rather old-fashioned style and a large size that drifts downstream with the current. In it sits an elderly woman with head bowed so that none can see her face. A few who have seen her, think that she is weeping, but others are not so sure.

Rather more modern is the ghost of Lyonshall. This is a charming little village strung out down a hillside in Herefordshire. In days gone by the village was served by a branch railway line that linked up with the main line at Leominster. The branch line has long gone, fallen victim to the transfer of passengers and freight to the roads, but the signs of its passing still remain.

Partway up the hill an embankment closes in on both sides of the road, ending in stone walls that crowd in and once formed the abutments for the bridge that carried the railway over the road. And to one side stands a rather curious house that has one door opening at street level and another on to the embankment. This building used to be the railway station, though it is now a private house.

The ghost of Lyonshall is to be seen standing or loitering alongside the road outside this former railway station. Those who have seen him say that he is rather elderly and gives the impression of being rather downtrodden or sad. Certainly he seems to be waiting for something. The story attached to this ghost is that he was a porter who worked here for many long years until his death in 1940. Thereafter he returned in spectral form to hang about

The ghost of Lyonshall frequents this stretch of road by the old railway station

outside the old station waiting for some passengers to arrive so that he could help them with their luggage.

One local is adamant that the old porter is not the only ghost thereabouts. He claims to have heard the distinctive sounds of an old steam train chugging down the now lifted lines from Leominster. The sounds were heard late on a still, summer's evening and were, the man says, quite clear and unmistakable. If so, it must have been a ghost for no trains run here these days.

Herefordshire is unusual in that it may have a haunting that can be tied directly to motor transport. In 2001 and 2002 a remarkable series of road accidents took place in the village of Stoke Lacy, where the A465 runs past the church. In less than 18 months no less than 26 cars ended up in the hedge or the ditch, depending on which side of the road they veered off.

At first the local council blamed speeding motorists. They installed new road signs, bollards with reflective strips and even had the road surface tested to check that it was not particularly slippery, but all to no avail. The accidents continued.

Mr Barrett, the farmer who owns the land on both sides of the road, and has to keep repairing his hedge and ditch, was reported in the local press as saying 'We haven't had that many accidents in the previous 40 years. I've seen three accidents myself and can't understand how they happen. Something needs to be done or someone is going to be killed as sure as night follows day.'

In fact one person has already been killed there in a motor accident. But that was back in the 1930s when a couple had an argument in their black Ford car as they drove through the village. Exactly what happened next is unclear, but some sort of a struggle occurred and the car crashed, killing the woman.

Strangely some of the motorists who have crashed here in recent times have reported that they felt as if somebody had suddenly grabbed their steering wheel and yanked it to one side. One man said the steering wheel had been pulled out of his hands by the force of the tug. Strangely, none of the accidents has involved cars travelling at any speed and none of those involved have been injured.

5 Echoes of War

Herefordshire has seen more than its fair share of fighting and warfare over the years. Lying as it does on the borders between England and Wales it has long been a focus for raiding and invasion. Indeed the very name Hereford means 'the ford of the army' in old English. The city of Hereford was put under serious siege no less than four times from 1055 to 1645. It is no wonder that war has left its mark so clearly in the spectral side of Herefordshire.

That said, one of the more active of the warlike shades to frequent the county is of fairly modern origin. Three miles north of Leominster stands Berrington Hall. This magnificent house was built by Henry Holland for Thomas Harley in 1781. The grounds were landscaped by Capability Brown and include a famous 14-acre lake.

During the Second World War the house was taken over by the army as a hospital for men invalided home from the front. It is to this period in its history that the ghost belongs. It is that of an infantryman in uniform, but without helmet or rifle. He is seen pottering about quietly and generally does little to draw attention to himself. It is presumed that the ghost is that of a soldier who died here of his wounds, but his precise identity is unknown.

Berrington Hall is now owned by the National Trust, which has lovingly restored the house and grounds to their original 1780s appearance. No amount of work has got rid of the ghost, however, who is still reported from time to time.

Rather more enigmatic are the ghosts that are seen on the banks of the river south of Pontrilas. Local tradition has it that the Duke of Monmouth won a great victory here. He is said to have raised his cap high over his head as a signal of victory, thus giving the name of Monmouth Cap to the place. Many people have assumed that this refers to an episode in the abortive rebellion led by the Protestant Duke of Monmouth in 1685 against his Catholic uncle King James II. But neither Monmouth nor his army got any closer to Herefordshire than the far side of Bristol, so the placename is more likely to have come from the fact that the famous Monmouth Cap (as worn at the Battle of Agincourt) was made here. Any battle fought in the vicinity must date back to medieval times when the Marcher Lords held sway in the area. Those semi-independent lords held the borders against Welsh raids, and fought not a few minor wars between themselves.

Whoever it was who fought here, their ghosts remain. They are seen marching about — some say they are dancing — by a mound that stands in a meadow close by the river.

Of rather more precise date is the ghost that marches through the countryside around Brampton Bryan Park. This is the ferocious and very angry ghost of Oliver Cromwell. During the Civil War of the 1640s, Brampton Bryan was one of the very few places in Herefordshire that declared for Parliament. Its owner, Sir Edward Harley, was a leading MP who staunchly opposed the more arbitrary aspects of the rule of King Charles I.

While he was in Westminster attending Parliament, Sir Edward left his home in the hands of his wife, Lady Brilliana Harley. It was this redoubtable lady who found herself under siege inside the castle in the spring of 1642. The Royalists lacked heavy guns, so Lady Harley and her men were able to hold out until April 1643.

The castle had been seriously damaged in the siege, so when the Civil War ended Sir Edward set about building a new house next door. Sir Edward's building work was almost complete when, on 3 September 1658, a terrible storm battered the estate. Trees were torn down, fences levelled and the incomplete house knocked about. A few days later news arrived from London that Oliver Cromwell had died on 3 September at about the time that the storm had struck. Sir Edward had fallen out with Cromwell in 1649 when he had refused Cromwell's demand that he should sign the king's death warrant.

The belief quickly grew that the storm had been caused by the Devil dragging Cromwell off to hell. A few days later Sir Edward wrote to a friend, 'I wish the devil had taken him any other way than through my park, for not content with doing me all the mischief he could when alive, he has knocked over some of my finest trees on his progress downwards.'

The tall man seen striding through the park in the autumn is generally reckoned to be the ghost of Oliver Cromwell. Locals take care not to approach the ghost, in case the Devil is close by.

The Civil War also left its spectral mark on Goodrich Castle, in tragic fashion. In 1643, the Earl of Stamford, who had seized Hereford in the interest of Parliament, garrisoned the castle. The tide of war moved on, and by 1645 Goodrich was occupied by a garrison led by the Royalist Sir Henry Lingen. Sometime in 1645 a new detachment of troops rode up led

The imposing walls of Goodrich Castle where a Civil War tragedy is thought to have led to a sad haunting

by a dashing young Herefordshire cavalier named Sir Charles Clifford, who brought his bride with him. The young woman was Alice Birch, the niece of a Parliamentarian commander named Colonel John Birch. Birch had won a reputation for ruthless and merciless violence during the war. The story goes that his niece had eloped with young Clifford rather than risk her uncle's wrath by asking permission to marry a Royalist.

By the summer of 1645 the king's cause was as good as lost after his two main armies had been defeated at the battles of Marston Moor and Naseby. Charles pinned his hopes on those strongholds still loyal to him holding out long enough for something to turn up. Goodrich was one such stronghold, and Lingen had orders to hold out for as long as possible.

In fact it was not until June 1646 that a Parliamentary army arrived. As fate would have it, it was Colonel Birch himself, along with Colonel Kyrle and 500 men on horse and foot, who came to Goodrich to win back the castle for Parliament; and thus Goodrich became the scene of one of the most desperate sieges in the Civil War. Birch's first attempt to capture the castle failed; the stables and outbuildings were burned, but the walls were not breached.

Then Colonel Birch took possession of a great culverin from Gloucester as well as other guns from Ludlow castle in the south of Shropshire. He even built a cannon that could carry a shell of two hundredweight, a massive siege mortar nicknamed 'Roaring Meg'. (The cannon until recently stood in the Churchill Gardens Museum in Hereford but it is now to be moved back to Goodrich, the scene of its triumph.)

For triumph, of course, it did. Even such sturdy walls as those at Goodrich could not withstand such a powerful weapon. Inside the castle, Lingen eyed the great mortar grimly. It was now just a matter of time. According to the rules of war as then understood, Lingen could surrender immediately on generous terms, or he could wait until the enemy had breached his walls, when he would be allowed to surrender and lead his men into captivity safe in the knowledge that their lives would be spared, but not much else. If he tried to hold out any longer, the attackers would be entitled to kill all defenders when they finally broke in. Lingen decided to surrender when his walls were breached, but to do everything he could to delay that time. He mounted raids at night, shot at the Parliamentarian gunners by day and tried all sorts of subterfuges. But the end result was not seriously in doubt.

For young Clifford and his wife, the prospects were bleak. They knew that Birch had been hunting for his niece and that he had found out with whom she had eloped. Birch had sworn dire revenge, and given his reputation few doubted that this would entail Clifford's failing to survive the siege. They seemed to be trapped, with no hope of escape.

But Colonel Lingen, sympathetic to their plight, agreed to help them. He arranged to give Clifford a horse and a bag of supplies, and to mount a diversion late one night so that the young cavalier could slip out of a postern gate and try to make his escape. That plan might have worked. But at the last minute, Alice decided to

The monument of Colonel Birch at Weobley ride with her husband.

At midnight the diversion began and the young couple rode out of the castle and down the hill towards a ford over the river. They made it as far as the riverbank, but then they were spotted by a Roundhead sentry who opened fire and called his comrades. Whether the destruction of Clifford and his young bridge was due to the water or the bullets was never clear, but the horse stumbled and threw its riders into the raging river, where they both drowned.

Goodrich Castle surrendered late in July. Birch sent his prisoners off to Bristol in chains. Then he used gunpowder to blast the defences of Goodrich to pieces and smash its roofs to make it uninhabitable. There is no record of his ever showing any emotion about the loss of his niece; presumably he considered her a traitor. His tomb in the church at Weobley is a grand affair of marble columns which carries a statue of him in full armour surrounded by the trophies of war.

Clifford and Alice may not have been granted such a memorial, but they were never forgotten, for their ghosts would not allow that to happen. The handsome young cavalier and his pretty wife have been glimpsed several times walking in or near Goodrich Castle where they spent their few months of happiness. They are also seen trying to ford the river, in which, whether the water is high or low, they seem to be struggling with a ferocious flood. Then the ghostly horse that they are riding rears and falls, after which all three ghosts vanish into the waters and are seen no more.

Exactly how old the ghostly knight of Bronsil Castle might be is unclear, though he would seem to date back to the Middle Ages. Whatever his age, the ghost first began walking in 1605, and did so with a persistence and noise that the castle's then owner, Gabriel Reede, found to be a great nuisance.

Reede consulted Master Allen, a local wizard of reputedly great power, to ask how to lay the ghost. Allen said that the

The ruins of Bronsil Castle which are haunted by an impressive ghostly knight

armoured ghost must be one of the Beauchamp family who had built the castle, and advised Reede to acquire one of their bones and put it somewhere inside Bronsil Castle. Reede promptly broke open the tomb of the first Lord Beauchamp — presumably John Beauchamp, who had died in 1475 — and removed a couple of vertebrae. These were taken to Bronsil and put in a wooden box on which was written 'The Bones of Lord Beauchamp'. The box was then placed in a locked cupboard.

The ghost duly stopped walking. In 1645 Bronsil Castle was captured by the Roundheads and burned. Only ruins remained. The escaping garrison took the box of Beauchamp's bones with them, and they remained in the new seat of the Reede's at New Court for some years, but were lost sometime in the 19th century.

Almost immediately the ghost began to walk again. Clanking around the few ruins of Bronsil that remain, the phantom figure is every inch the ghostly knight. Unfortunately for modern day ghost hunters the last firm sighting of him was back in the 1930s. Perhaps his powers have finally gone.

No such deterioration in power has affected the phantom of Sir Thomas Vaughan, better known as Black Vaughan because of his wickedness and evil deeds. This imposing man was killed at the Battle of Banbury, one of the battles of the Wars of the Roses fought in 1469. His tomb, a magnificent work in alabaster, can be seen in Kington church.

During his lifetime, Black Vaughan was notorious for his vicious temper, readiness to resort to violence and his blatant dishonesty. Vaughan fought on the side of the Lancastrians, the ruling faction which was notoriously corrupt and whose leaders siphoned off government funds to line their own pockets. No wonder Vaughan joined them. Bad as Vaughan's behaviour was for the area around Kington, it was as nothing to what followed his death.

First to appear was Black Vaughan's hunting hound, which had vanished when its master died. The dog returned in spectral form to pad around the lanes, howling in a dismal and terrifying fashion. Some weeks later, the ghost of Black Vaughan himself began to be seen. Most often he stood beneath an old oak tree gazing out across the acres that had been his in life.

It was not long before his phantom became more active. A favourite trick of his was to leap up behind a rider, grab the reins and set off on a terrifying cross-country ride. The horse invariably came to grief at some point, usually trying to leap a hedge or wall too tall for it to manage. The unfortunate rider would be cast to the ground. If he were lucky he would escape with cuts and bruises, but some suffered broken bones. Another of Black Vaughan's tricks was to appear as a gigantic black bull, then charge at passersby. Many a cart was overturned when the horses bolted when attacked by the spectral bull.

So often did these unpleasant and terrifying things occur that at last the locals called on their priest to rid them of the ghost. The vicar, whose name is not recorded, did not feel up to the daunting task if for no other reason than that he was notoriously fond of a glass of wine and thought he might not be sufficiently holy to deal with the powerful Black Vaughan. He therefore sent for eleven other vicars to gather in Kington to help him perform the ceremony.

On the appointed night the twelve clergymen gathered by Black Vaughan's oak tree. Each man brought with him a Bible and a candle, while the host vicar had a silver snuffbox as well. Almost as soon as the vicars began to read from their Bibles, the ghost of Black Vaughan appeared. Taking the form of himself, then that of the bull, he stormed around the sacred circle. Then he called up his phantom hound to help him defeat the vicars.

One by one each candle went out as the vicar holding it was reduced to silence by the demonic power of Black Vaughan. Eventually the only vicar left reading was the habitually drunk vicar of Kington himself.

'Why art thou so fierce?' he called to Vaughan.

'I was fierce when I was a man', the ghost replied. 'But now I am a devil.'

The vicar carried on reading. Then Black Vaughan gave a terrible howl and was sucked into the snuffbox.

'Anywhere, anywhere but the Red Sea', the ghost screamed as the lid was snapped shut on him.

The demon dog had to be caught next. Emboldened by his success, the bibulous vicar approached the dog with a collar and chain while continuing to read from the Bible. As meek as a puppy, the dog allowed itself to be chained.

Eager to be rid of the demonic pair as quickly as possible, the vicar of Kington looked around for a handy place to confine the phantoms for the standard thousand years. His eyes fell on the pond outside Hergest Court. Hurriedly attaching the dog's chain to the snuffbox, he tossed both into the pond.

That was some 400 years ago, maybe more. And it would seem that the good vicar's exorcism is beginning to wear out. Perhaps Black Vaughan is more powerful than was thought. In the 1930s his ghost began to be seen striding around the pond. The demon dog has been seen trotting in the same area, a chain clanking behind him. Perhaps most ominously, a ghostly bull was seen near the church. In the 1980s the then owner of Hergest decided to fill in the pond. He had actually got the workmen on site and the bulldozer revved up when a string of bubbles broke the surface of the pond, turning it into a mini maelstrom of waves and froth. The owner suspended the work — just in case — although it has since been completed.

Famous as Black Vaughan was, and is, round Kington, his fame is strictly local. Not so that of the man who haunts Croft Castle. This tall man walks around the castle dressed in a leather doublet and leather riding gear that seems to date him to the 15th century. He is usually identified as Owen Glendower, or Owain Glyndwr, though why is not entirely obvious.

Glyndwr was born in Montgomeryshire in around 1350 to a family of gentry that claimed descent from the old royal family of Gwynedd. He trained as a lawyer in London and was embarking on a moderately successful career when events back home intervened. His family got into a dispute with Lord Grey over some complex property issues. Grey was a favourite of King Henry IV, so the Glyndwrs were unable to enforce their rights although the law seemed to be on their side.

Glyndwr raised his men and harried Grey's lands. What began as a minor local scuffle quickly developed into a wider Welsh rebellion against the imposition of English laws in place of the traditional Welsh legal system. Glyndwr proclaimed himself Prince of Wales and, in 1402, formed an alliance with a northern English rebellion against Henry.

The alliance came to grief at the Battle of Shrewsbury in 1403, but Glyndwr continued to maintain his independence. Aided by a force of soldiers sent by the King of France, he held out in the wilds of Wales for years. Sometime around 1416 he vanished, most believe to somewhere along the border of Herefordshire and Wales, as his daughter had married one of the Scudamores, but his ultimate fate is unknown.

Quite why he should return to Croft Castle in spectral form is not known, although he did have a connection with the castle, as his daughter Janet married John Croft. It is therefore quite likely that he came this way, though there is no certain documentation that he ever did. But whether the tall ghostly man in leather is Glyndwr or not, it is certainly seen quite often.

Older still than Glyndwr is the ghost that lurks around Burrington. In 1066 this manor was home to a wealthy landowner named Edric of Wenlock. For some reason, this Edric did not march to fight at the Battle of Hastings; perhaps he was tasked by King Harold with guarding the Welsh frontiers. For whatever reason, Edric survived the general slaughter of English nobles at Hastings.

When William the Conqueror was crowned King of England he sent messengers out to men such as Edric asking for their oath of loyalty. William also sent to Herefordshire a force of knights and workmen with orders to build and garrison a castle at Hereford. In the summer of 1067 the Norman knights rode to attack the home of Edric as he had not yet given his oath. Edric responded by raising his men to march on Hereford, where they burned down the half-completed castle. Thereafter the Normans left Edric alone.

Then, in 1070, Edric rose in rebellion once more. This time he marched alongside Prince Bleddyn of Gwynedd and Prince Rhiwallon of Powys, the two most powerful rulers in Wales. Edric captured Shrewsbury, then swept on to Stafford. From there he marched on Nottingham, but was met by King William and the main Norman army somewhere on the road. The battle ended in victory for the Normans, but that victory was not total. Edric and many of his men survived. They began a guerrilla war against the Normans from the forests of Herefordshire that lasted for years. It was at this time that Edric earned his nickname of 'the Wild'.

Sometime after 1075, Edric the Wild made his peace with William. That the Herefordshire man had not been defeated is shown by the fact that he agreed generous terms and was allowed to regain his former estates. He was alive in 1086 when his name appears on a legal document, but the date of his death is unknown.

His ghost rides around the Burrington area in magnificent style. He gallops over the fields with his warlike band at his back, all mounted on spirited chargers and armed to the teeth. Sometimes he rides through the skies, shrieking his wild war cries so loud as to strike terror into all those who hear him.

The Queen's Arms in Hereford's Broad Street is home to a spectre that is much older than the pub

One of the nameless followers of Edric the Wild still apparently resides quietly in, of all places, the comfortable bar of the Queen's Arms in Hereford's Broad Street. The building is nowhere near old enough to harbour such an ancient phantom, though it is possible that it stands on the foundations of a very much older structure.

Older still than Edric and his men are the ghostly horsemen who ride around Bunshill. Back in the 7th century Herefordshire was ruled by King Herla, a Welsh ruler descended from one of the old families of the Romano-Britons who were still struggling to hold back the English invaders.

On the day of King Herla's wedding to the daughter of the King of Franks, a strange rider came to his court. The man was richly dressed, but short and ugly. He asked permission to attend King Herla's wedding along with his entourage, and said that in return he would invite Herla and his companions to his own wedding, due to be held a year and a day later. Herla agreed.

Up rode a large and magnificent company of men and ladies, all dressed in the most magnificent clothes and riding beautiful horses. Clearly these were the fairy folk, and Herla realised that he must treat them with care and great respect. This he did, serving them with the finest foods and wines he could muster and seating them in places of honour. King Herla sent them home laden with gifts.

Exactly a year later the fairy king returned to invite King Herla to his wedding. Riding off with an entourage of his bravest warriors, Herla followed. The fairy king led them to a cave entrance in the hills just outside Bunshill. Riding in, the column of horsemen passed through caves and tunnels lit by flaming torches. Eventually the riders emerged into a broad, beautiful valley. The fairy king lodged Herla and his men in a magnificent pavilion for the night, and the next day the wedding of the fairy king took place in great splendour. That night Herla and his men stayed again at the pavilion

The Wye at Bunshill where the enigmatic horsemen of King Herla have been seen

and on the third day they prepared to ride home. The fairy king thanked Herla for visiting, then gave each of the men a fine gift. To Herla he gave a bloodhound puppy, saying 'Now take care on your return. Neither you nor your men must dismount until this puppy first jumps down.' With that he led Herla back through the caves and tunnels to re-emerge at Bunshill.

Herla and his men set off for home, but they soon lost their way. It seemed as if the familiar landmarks had changed. Seeing a lone peasant at work in the woods, Herla called out to him and asked the way. The peasant stared at him blankly, then began to speak in faltering Welsh.

'Lord, I hardly understood you,' the man said. 'You are speaking Welsh and I am English. I know a few words of your language only. Who are you and what do you seek?'

'I am King Herla,' replied Herla, wondering what an Englishman was doing in his lands. 'I seek the way to my palace.'

The Englishman rubbed his chin. 'Herla?' he said. 'I recall that there was a king of that name some two centuries ago. He was the last king of the Welsh to rule Herefordshire. Folk do say that he and all his finest warriors vanished into a cave hereabouts and never came back. We English came in when Herla was gone, taking the land with ease as all the Welsh warriors were gone with their king.'

Herla was, naturally, astonished. One of his men leapt down from his horse to grab the Englishman, but the moment his feet touched the ground he crumpled to dust. Herla remembered the warning of the fairy king and forbade any man to dismount until the dog jumped down.

From that day on King Herla and his men have ridden the hills around Bunshill. They are searching, or so the story has it, for the entrance back to the fairy kingdom in the hope that the fairy king can put things right.

Such is the old story. What can be said with some accuracy is that ghostly horsemen have been reported trotting around Bunshill.

Before the time of Herla, in the murky dark ages around the year 500 or so, Herefordshire was firmly in the hands of the Romano-Britons and the English were pinned into coastal enclaves far to the east in Kent, Norfolk and Northumberland. Those were the days of King Arthur, who ruled the crumbling government of Roman Britain as it descended slowly into chaos.

Arthur does not seem to have been a Herefordshire man. Most believe that he came from somewhere to the east, growing up in a place that was subsequently lost to the English so that its precise location has been lost. But local legend has it that he came to Herefordshire often, and his ghost remains.

The stretch of road to the south of Hoarwithy where the ghosts of King Arthur and his men have been seen

The best place to spot the phantom of King Arthur is along a stretch of the River Wye known locally as the Red Rail, near the village of Hoarwithy. It is here that he rides with a dozen or so companions as if out for a day's hunting.

Exactly who Arthur was is a matter of great debate, though there seems little reason to believe — as do some academics — that he never existed. The few references to him that can be taken as having any real historic value make him a war leader and a ruler whose parents were Romano-British landowners. Beyond that all is shadows. It seems likely, however, that he had some sort of control over the princelings and town authorities who exercised local power in post-Roman Britain. The nature and extent of that control is unclear, other than that he led their men to war and won the Battle of Badon Hill sometime between 490 and 520 — dates are exasperatingly difficult to pin down in this era.

Bizarre as it may seem, there is rather more information available about the wizard Merlin than about Arthur. Lurking behind the later stories of magic and mysticism lies the very real figure of Myrddin Wyllt. This bard, poet and prophet was driven mad when he witnessed the slaughter of the Battle of Arfderydd in 573 when the Britons of Strathclyde defeated those of Gwenddoleu in a nasty war that opened the way to English invasion of what is now northwestern England.

Arthur's Stone, above Dorstone, said by some to be where King Arthur
fought one of his battles

Already a famous poet, Myrddin's subsequent wanderings, ravings and prophetic gibberings ensured him a place in legend. Later generations claimed that he had foretold all sorts of historic events. He was later grafted on to the story of Arthur as the latter was developed into an almost mythical figure in 12th century romantic literature.

One of the places in Herefordshire to which Myrddin Wyllt is said to have come in his mad wanderings is Longtown Castle. Indeed, he is said to be buried just east of the castle and to haunt the spot. If anyone should encounter a shambling ghostly figure clad in rags, they should address him in Welsh. The mad prophet may then foretell the future for them.

On the Doward, a hill near Symonds Yat, lies Merlin's Cave. When this cavern was excavated in the 1920s, it was found to contain a large amount of animal bones dating back to the last ice age, plus a burial of ancient but uncertain date. There was also a heavily worn Roman coin of the emperor Constantine the Great. Given the date of the coin and its worn condition, it would seem to have been dropped around the year 500. This is a bit early for Merlin, but it shows that somebody was using the cave in the post-Roman era.

Not far away lies King Arthur's Cave, actually two linked caverns. When this was excavated it was found to contain masses of material from the Stone Age and Bronze Age, but nothing much from more recent times and certainly nothing to link it to King Arthur.

Arthur's Stone stands on Merbach Hill above Dorstone. It is a stone age burial chamber made of gigantic sarsen boulders that were once covered by an

The old Roman road to Kenchester where spectral legionnaires are said to march

earth mound, though this has since eroded away. Local legend has it that Arthur fought a single combat here with a rival king, or with a giant in another version of the tale. Arthur won and buried his vanquished rival here.

The monument itself is much, much older than the date for Arthur, but that does not mean that the stories are false. Ancient landmarks such as this tumble-down burial chamber were often used as venues for fairs, mustering points for armies and other purposes. A single combat at such a site is not only likely but has been recorded numerous times in history. That said, there is no real evidence that Arthur ever came here.

Older still are the soldiers who march at Kenchester on the nights of the full moon. These are Roman soldiers who march in column with measured tread along the route of the old Roman road that leads to what was, in the 3rd century, a small walled town called *Magnis*. Back in the 18th century a cache of Roman coins was found here and dubbed fairy money. The little people were traditionally said to live among the ruins.

Possibly even older are the shadowy phantoms of Twyn-y-beddau, a couple of miles south of Hay-on-Wye. Piles of human bones have been found on this bleak hillside and local legend has it that they are the remains of men killed in some great battle of long ago. No recorded battle ever took place here, so it must have been an ancient battle indeed.

6 Animal Hauntings

No matter which of the various theories to account for ghosts to which one subscribes, it is difficult to account for animal hauntings. They are, it must be confessed, something of a puzzle. That Herefordshire has more ghostly animals that most counties is a fact, and one which makes the supernatural side of the county especially fascinating.

There are those who believe that ghosts are the souls of the dead condemned by some higher power to walk the earth as their sins make them unfit to move on. But what sins can animals commit? Others hold that ghosts are the souls of the troubled dead bound to some earthly spot by a guilty conscience or in the hope of righting old wrongs or revealing some hidden valuable. Again, ghosts of animals scarcely seem to fit into this explanation.

Many researchers believe that hauntings are caused when walls, stones and rocks somehow record an event. This recording can then be played back when the conditions are right. Exactly how such recordings are made is unknown. However, the fact that so many ghosts are linked to violent death, disastrous love affairs and the like has led some to speculate that intense emotions are involved somehow. Do animals have emotions? Probably, but whether they are intense enough to cause a haunting is not easy to know.

Certainly something about animals can trigger a haunting, and that something seems more likely to occur in Herefordshire than anywhere else. Take, for instance, the strange story of the Burghill hog. Back in the early 19th century, what is now the A4110 was then a major coaching route running north from Hereford toward Knighton and Shrewsbury. The road climbs up north of Hereford near the village of Burghill, and here a ghostly pig was seen several times in the later 19th century. On the crest of the hill there used to stand an elm tree, beneath which the phantom Burghill hog used to be seen. The great pig, for it was a massive porker, used to be seen behaving as if it were tethered to the tree. It would watch approaching humans with some apprehension and then back away as if seeking shelter beneath the tree's spreading branches. Then it would fade from view.

No story ever seems to have become attached to this odd spectre, though it was seen often enough. The tree has now sadly gone the way of so many that fell victim to Dutch elm disease in the 1980s, and, alas, the ghostly hog has gone too.

One phantom animal that it is well to avoid is the generic gigantic black hound that goes by various names. In Herefordshire these creatures sometimes go by their Welsh name of cwm annwn, though in England they are more generally known as the black shuck. This awesome apparition usually takes the form of a gigantic black dog with shaggy fur. It is sometimes the size of a large hound, but can on occasion be as big as a donkey or pony, and sometimes even larger. If its sheer size were not remarkable enough, the shuck has eyes that are perfectly round, not oval like those of most creatures. At times these distinctive eyes may glow red with an inner fire.

Meeting such a creature would be unnerving enough, but the shuck is widely held to be a harbinger of bad luck, even of death. Merely seeing the huge hound may be enough to bring misfortune, but if the dog looks you in the eye then some seriously sad event is almost certain to be imminent. It is for this reason that those who see the shuck approaching are advised to turn their eyes aside until it has passed by.

The cwm annwn which frequents the lanes near Clodock church cannot be so easily avoided. It delights in trotting alongside pedestrians, and will positively speed beside cars and vans. It seems able to keep up with any vehicle, though it does not seem to do more than trot along no matter how fast it is moving. This hound is seen most often about half a mile away from the church, loping uphill in unearthly silence.

The lane outside Clodock church is the venue for one of the most terrifying animal ghosts in Herefordshire

A whole pack of the cwm annwn hounds may be seen on occasion at Parton Cross, near Eardisley. These dogs trot ominously around the countryside, sometimes heading over toward Pembridge. At Pembridge itself only a lone dog is seen, the rest of the pack presumably having gone elsewhere.

When a new vicar took over the parish of Kington in 1845, he was told by the good folk of that town that the great black hounds appeared only when a wicked person was about to die. They were, he was told, the hunting hounds of the Devil himself sent to hunt down the soul of the damned person and drag it back to Hell. Needless to say the vicar did not hold with such superstitions, but the stories have persisted.

Although the dogs are considered evil and often linked to the Devil, they have a strange liking for holy places such as churches, chapels and springs dedicated to ancient saints. They also tend to hover around old stone circles, henges and burial mounds.

These cwm annwn or black shuck hounds are interesting creatures. They are known right across Britain, but do not seem to put in much of an appearance elsewhere in the world. Some ghost hunters have speculated that these massive hounds are, in fact, some half-remembered relic of the old pre-Christian religion of Britain. Many Christian churches were built on pagan sites, while sacred springs were dedicated to old deities long before the medieval saints took them over.

It was typical of the early Christian missionaries to these islands that they sought both to take over old sites and festivals while at the same time demonising the gods they celebrated. It is perfectly possible that the cwm annwn was originally a dog sacred to one of the old pagan gods. The Christian arrivals would have denounced him as a work of Satan, hence his modern links to the Devil and to bad luck.

Whatever the truth, the shuck is obviously a powerful entity. He is seen in widely distant places at fairly frequent intervals. Maybe he still retains some of his pagan power.

Some researchers believe that the strength and frequency of a phantom apparition depends directly on how many people believe in it and how strongly they hold that belief. The actual percipient need not believe in the ghost — indeed they need not even know that it is supposed to exist — it is enough that a large number of other people believe in it.

Some interesting experiments into this theory have been undertaken. The best known took place in 1972 in Toronto, Canada, when a group of psychical researchers decided to believe in the ghost of a 17th-century English aristocrat named Philip. The group invented a long, complex life story for 'Philip' based on real places and events in Diddington, Warwickshire, around the year 1640 — although the main character of Philip was entirely ficti-tious. They met for several weeks, sitting around a table and concentrating on 'Philip' and his imaginary life.

Before long the group began to receive spectral messages from 'Philip' by way of coded raps on the table or walls of the room where they met. 'Philip' would answer questions, confirming the imaginary story or filling in gaps that had been left. The details that Philip gave were often wildly inac-curate from an historical point of view, but were internally consistent with the invented story.

There are many unanswered questions about the Philip Experiment and similar investigations. It may be that the group somehow created the spirit, or that some mischievous spirit latched on to their plans and played a trick. Whatever the truth, the events do seem to indicate that it may be possible for the power of human thought and belief to create a spectral entity — such as the cwm annwn of Herefordshire.

One of the great black hounds has a rather complex story attached to it, unlike the others which simply roam the countryside on some vaguely defined evil business. This is the great black dog of Hoarwithy.

Back in the 1860s or thereabouts, a Hoarwithy farmhand named Tom Reece was walking back to Hoarwithy after a pre-Christmas night out with friends in Ross. As he strolled down the lane he heard soft, padding footsteps behind him and saw a large black dog loping down the lane toward him. Tom stood to one side to let the dog pass, but it stopped as it drew closer. When Tom continued on his way, the dog fell in with him keeping a few paces behind.

At this point Tom thought that the dog was a natural creature and although he did not recognise it, thought it must belong to some local farm or other. After a while Tom, who had been drinking, got fed up with the dog. He shouted at it, but it took no notice. He threw a stick at it, but the dog merely regarded him with a quizzical expression. Then Tom picked up a fallen branch and stepped forward as if to hit the dog. The hound then sprang back out of his reach and suddenly took on human form — it was Tom's long-dead father.

Tom fled the scene and hurried home. He arrived in a terrible state of agitation. While he told his family about the dog, he did not mention the appearance of his father's ghost. The weeks passed and Tom grew steadily more depressed and lethargic.

Then one night he suddenly got up in the middle of the night and woke his brother, who slept in the same room. 'I have got to go out,' he told his brother. 'Don't worry about me' — words that were guaranteed to make the brother deeply worried.

Tom apparently felt a strong impulse to go to some nearby woods. Once in the shadow of the trees he again saw the phantom hound, and followed it. When the dog stopped, it again changed into the ghost of his father and pointed to the ground. 'Dig!' commanded the ghost. Tom dug and quickly discovered a leather bag. 'Throw it in the Wye!' the ghost ordered, and Tom duly did so.

On the instant that the bag disappeared under the waters the ghost vanished, and Tom fainted. When he awoke it was to find the chill dawn of winter creeping over the landscape and a heavy frost all round. Tom sat up, his body chilled to the bone, but his depression lifted. He never again saw either the dog or his father and never again suffered depression.

A ghostly hound of a rather different kind haunts Hampton Court, near Leominster, a castle built by Sir Rowland Lenthall in the 1420s. Sir Rowland had been born into a fairly humble family, but had been knighted by King Henry V for his bravery during the Battle of Agincourt. He gained the Hampton estates when he later married the daughter of the Earl of Arundel and decided to build himself a castle to match his new status in life.

By this date the firepower of the rapidly developing cannon was making old-style castles redundant as serious fortifications, and although the castle that Lenthall built had its crenallations and towers, it was in reality more of a comfortable country house than a fortress. In 1510 the family sold the castle and estates to the Coningsby family, and it is with them that the haunting began.

The Coningsby family had a hound as one of their emblems and hounds feature prominently in a painting that one of the family commissioned some 300 years ago. The castle and grounds soon began to play host to a phantom dog, said to be guarding the place for the Coningsby family. When the family

Hampton Court, built by one of the victors of Agincourt and now home to a phantom hound

53

sold up in the 19th century to the Arkwrights, who had made a fortune from the industrial revolution, they left behind the painting of the hounds.

The painting still hangs in the house and bad luck of the worst kind is said to be the fate of any owner of the castle who allows it to be removed. Today the castle is the home for a charitable trust and is not open to the general public, though the magnificent gardens are accessible and you can take tea in the fine tearoom. And you may catch a glimpse of the hound trotting about.

At Hergest there is said to be a gigantic black hound dragging a rattling chain. This dreadful beast is the hell hound owned by Black Vaughan, whose story is told in the chapter entitled Echoes of War.

It is a cat that forms the centre of an odd story from Eaton Bishop. Back in the 1820s, a young man came home after a day's hunting with a curious story to tell. He had been out on the hills when a mist came down and he lost his way. He saw a light and walked toward it hoping it was a cottage where he could ask for directions. Instead the light turned out to be the burning torches carried by a procession of cats. Those in the centre carried a small coffin on which was set a tiny crown and sceptre. As the young man reached this point in his story, the family cat suddenly sprang up from where it had been dozing

The church at Mordiford which was once decorated with a painting of the dreadful Mordiford dragon

by the fireside. 'Aha,' called out the cat. 'Old Peter is dead. Then I am King of the Cats,' and he bolted up the chimney never to be seen again.

Until the church at Mordiford was repaired in 1821, the Mordiford Dragon was painted prominently on the outside of the church facing toward the Wye so that travellers approaching the village over the long bridge would get a good view of it.

According to a local legend a village girl named Maud one day found a tiny dragon, about the size of a cucumber, in the nearby woods and took it home. Her father warned her it was dangerous and told her to get rid of it. The girl, however, made it a small nest nearby and fed it regularly on milk. The small dragon grew rapidly and soon it was taking chickens and rabbits as food. From that it progressed to sheep, cattle and even humans. Maud alone could approach it safely, but even she could not persuade it to leave Mordiford.

Eventually a man named Garston offered to kill the monster in return for a rich reward. He armed himself with a sword, then built a huge wooden barrel from which emerged numerous spikes, blades and hooks. He carried the barrel down to the spot on the Wye where the beast was accustomed to drink. Then he climbed into the barrel.

When the monster approached, Garston shouted insults at it. He then ducked down into the barrel and slammed the lid shut. The dragon pounced, but every time it attacked the barrel it injured itself on the blades. Finally, when the dragon was weakened through loss of blood, Garston leapt out and killed it with his sword. The spectral beast is still to be seen, at times when the mist rises from the Wye, writhing in its death agonies.

A most peculiar ghost is to be seen near Weobley. A farmer on the estates of Garnstone Park committed suicide and came back in the shape of a ghostly calf. For some reason this phantom can be seen only by those born during the hours of darkness. Why the unfortunate man should adopt the shape of a young cow nobody seems to know, nor is it clear why the ghostly calf is linked to the farmer at all. It may, after all, be nothing more than a ghostly calf.

The ghost that haunts the River Lugg near Marden is not, strictly speaking, that of an animal — but nor is it that of a human.

Back in medieval times the good folk of Marden commissioned a bell for their church. It was brought up the Wye, then the Lugg, by barge. As the bell was being unloaded a mermaid of fearsome aspect — some said she was a water demon — sprang from the Lugg, grabbed the bell and dragged it down into the river, declaring that it would never sound out from Marden Church.

The villagers threw in grappling hooks in an attempt to retrieve their expensive bell, but to no avail. They then consulted the local wizard. He advised them that there was only one way to defeat the magical powers of the mermaid. First they had to find twelve white freemartins — cows that had not yet given birth to a calf. These then had to be yoked to a harness of yew and driven by men armed with wands of wittern, or mountain ash. Above all the bell had to be retrieved without a word being spoken by any of the men involved.

The River Lugg at Marden is home to an unusual and rather belligerent apparition

Having rounded up twelve white freemartins from the surrounding villages, the men of Marden went down to the Lugg. The grappling hooks were again cast into the river, the ropes being attached to the elm yokes. The wittern wands were then employed and the cattle took up the strain.

Slowly, inch by inch, the bell began to be dragged from the water. As it broke the surface, it was seen to contain the mermaid herself, curled up and fast asleep. Agonisingly slowly the bell was hauled out of the river until it hung poised on the bank. One of the men, forgetting the injunction about silence, called out:

> In spite of all the devils in hell,
> Now we'll land the Marden bell.

At this the mermaid woke up. Staring round angrily she at once realised what was happening. Cutting the ropes she pushed the bell back into the river, chanting:

If it had not been
for your wittern wands
And your yew-tree pins
I'd have had your twelve freemartins in.

With a final laugh she was gone.

The bell never was recovered. It is still possible to hear it rolling around on the river bed, tolling slowly as it rocks from side to side. The mermaid is seen too, gambolling lightly in the river and splashing about. She is said to be exceptionally attractive, and does not have the fishy tail of her marine counterparts. But she is best avoided for she is not well disposed to humans.

The story is interesting on many levels. Some think that it is an echo of the times when Christianity first came to the area, as many rivers are thought to have had a pagan goddess linked to them. The mermaid may be this half-forgotten deity. If so, it would explain her hostility to a Christian church bell for the sound of a church bell has long been believed to have the power to drive away demons, and a pagan goddess would be included in that category.

There is an odd footnote to the Marden story. In 1848 a farmer was clearing out an old pond with a view to reshaping it. Buried deep in the mud was an ancient bell. This was no great church bell, but a handbell. It was clearly very old, so the man took it to Hereford Museum, where it remains. The bell was made of four bronze plates riveted together to form a square bell. The clapper is missing, but the loop where it hung is still there. It is thought that the bell is at least a thousand years old.

The church at Marden, still without its mighty bell, stands on the banks of the Lugg

Perhaps some ancient Christian missionary once

came to convert the pagan folk of Marden, carrying with him this prayer bell. Was he overcome by the adherents of the local water goddess, and his Christian bell sacrificed to her as a token of the victory of paganism, albeit only a temporary one?

7   Wayside Spooks

If the popular imagination prefers to put ghosts into stately homes, ruined castles and churchyards, it is interesting that some of the most active ghosts are to be found flitting about in the fresh air beside the roads, lanes and footpaths that crisscross Herefordshire.

One of the more gruesome, and spectacular, of these is the ghostly inn of Callow. Most phantoms are of single humans, sometimes of two and very occasionally more. But Callow musters an entire ghostly inn complete with staff and customers.

This is no ordinary inn, but one that was demolished many years ago due to the horrible crimes committed there. The A49 now bypasses the village, but the old road into the village from the south passes the site of this inn, shortly before it reaches the church. The inn was a welcoming one, serving fine ales, ciders and good food. Many travellers on their way to or from Hereford stopped here and enjoyed themselves enormously.

A few visitors found when they got home that they had lost a valuable possession of some kind. It was never anything much and most people thought that they must have dropped their watch, purse or the odd coin somewhere along the way. In fact, the landlord of the Callow Inn was adept at filching things from his guests. He was careful not to take too much in case investigations led back to his inn.

But he could be more ambitious. If a particularly wealthy gentleman should stay, the landlord would put his attractive wife on the case. Flashing her bright eyes and making a fuss of the visitor she would wheedle information out of him. In particular she would want to know if he was travelling alone and, if so, whether any of his friends or family knew that he was staying at the Callow Inn. If they did she would quickly be called away to another customer.

But if the man was alone and nobody knew his travel plans, his fate was sealed. He would be plied with fine wines until he was tipsy, then tucked up in bed. When the inn had emptied, the landlord would sneak upstairs to murder the guest and rob him of everything he had. Then the landlord and his wife would carry the body away across two fields to be buried in a hidden copse.

Eventually a man was missed and his trail was followed to the Callow Inn, but no further. Investigations were made and soon a list of unsolved vanishings was revealed. Exactly how many travellers had been murdered was never discovered. One was enough to hang the miscreants, and hanged they were.

But they return in spectral form to Callow. Most often the ghosts of the murderers are seen staggering alongside the old main road carrying a corpse between them. They are seen only on moonlit nights. More rarely the long demolished inn is also seen, its windows filled with a warm, welcoming light. Fortunately it vanishes if anyone seeks to approach.

The lane that runs from Hereford to Weobley goes past the entrance driveway of Wormsley Grange. It is around these gates that two imposing spectres are to be seen. They appear sometimes together and at other times separately.

The first phantom is that of a pretty young lady dressed in a long silk gown that seems to place her in the late 18th century. She wears a beautiful jewelled necklace and her fingers are heavy with rings. The second ghost

The old towers of Wormsley Grange stand at the end of a long drive.
Both drive and towers are haunted by an elegant ghostly couple

is that of a tall gentleman dressed all in black and wearing a tall hat with a narrow brim. The ghosts linger by the gates, then turn away from the road to walk up to the house. Although nobody seems to know who these ghosts are, it is widely believed that they can be seen only by those born between 11pm and 1am, that is around the time of midnight. An odd pair, it must be said.

Altogether more straightforward in a ghostly sense is the lady who rides her horse along the B4362 near Yarpole. She rides a prancing grey mount which trots along the centre of the road to the consternation of motorists who come across her suddenly. Some say that in the 19th century she was exorcised into Haugh Pool, but if so, she must have overcome the powers of the clergy to return to her old haunts.

The bridge that carries the lane out of the charming village of Eardisland crosses the tranquil River Arrow. The bridge is said to be haunted by some phantom of awesome power. This ghost, it is claimed, can cause horses to bolt, cars to break down and pedestrians to flee in blind panic. Perhaps fortunately, it has not been encountered for some time.

Another haunted bridge is that which crosses the River Monnow from Kentchurch to Llangua, in Wales. The ghosts that are seen here are dancing their way over the bridge. Some people have described them as being the phantoms of half a dozen finely dressed gentlemen accompanied by an equal number of beautiful ladies. Others think that these apparitions are fairy folk. Either way, it is probably best not to interfere with them.

Equally enigmatic are the three ghosts of the High Street in Ross. They appear, stomp along the pavement for a few seconds then vanish. So far as

A whole group of dancing phantoms cross the bridge over the River Monnow from Kentchurch to Llangua

can be discovered, nobody has got close enough to discover who they are, still less why they return to the street.

Just outside St Weonards once stood a haunted megalith beside the road, though its location is now uncertain. The events that led to the haunting took place many years ago, but these stories can be frustratingly vague about dates which makes them almost impossible to pin down through local records.

Apparently, at the time (whenever it was), the local farmers were suffering an outbreak of sheepstealing. Since no strangers had been seen in the area, it was assumed that some local man was making off with them. And since no local flocks were increasing in number, the sheep were assumed to end up being killed and taken to some unscrupulous butcher in Ross, Monmouth or Hereford. Whoever the thief was, he was careful, for no amount of watching by shepherds ever caught him out.

Then one dawn a farmhand leaving St Weonards to walk to work found a gruesome sight. Hanging from the standing stone was a well known local wastrel. He was stone dead, suspended by his neck in a most curious fashion. The dead man was obviously the sheep stealer, for some time the night before he had clearly killed a sheep. Tying the hind legs of the sheep together, the man had slung the animal over his back, with the rope connecting its hind legs strung around his neck. He must have stopped at the standing stone to take a rest and placed the dead sheep on top of the stone. The sheep had then fallen off the stone, yanking the rope tight and jerking the man off his feet to strangle slowly to death.

It is perhaps hardly surprising that the ghost of the unfortunate thief should return to lurk along the roadside around the standing stone. He does not seem to do much, but simply stands and gazes balefully at passersby.

Another criminal lurks, or rather lurked, about White Cross, an impressive landmark on the road running northwest out of Hereford. His crime was to have moved boundary marker stones to increase the size of his land and reduce that of a neighbour. In 1876 the *Hereford Times* told the story.

> There was Old Taylor's ghost, that used to walk about the White Cross. He couldn't rest, because he had moved a landmark. He used to ride upon a little pony, and sometimes he would be seen sitting on a stile. I have never seen old Taylor myself, but have heard many say that they had seen him. At last his ghost was laid. One stormy night a fellow walked into the bar of the Nag's Head, and said he had seen Old Taylor, and had promised to meet him in the Morning Pits that night at twelve. Of course nobody believed him, and as the night wore on the others jeered at him and said 'I would not go on such a night as this'. He said he would not; but as the hour drew near he was obliged

to go. Something forced him to run, so that he reached the Morning Pits as the clock struck twelve. There the old man was waiting.

'Follow me' said he.

The [man] followed him into some strange place, which they seemed to reach in a very short time. In the place were two immense stones. 'Take up these stones,' said Old Taylor.

'I can't' says Denis (he was nicknamed Denis the Liar).

'You can', said Taylor, 'try'. He tried, and lifted the stones easily. 'Now come with me', said Taylor, 'and place them where I shall show you'.

He carried them and put them down with ease. 'Now,' said Old Taylor, 'I caution you never tell anybody what you see here this night'. Denis promised. 'And now,' said Old Taylor, 'lie down on your face and as you value your life don't attempt to look either way until you hear music, and then get away as fast as you can.'

Denis lay a long time without hearing what he earnestly desired, but at last the welcome sound of music was heard. Denis the liar was a different man after that, though he soon died from the effects of the night.

As recounted in the newspaper, the story of Old Taylor has several elements familiar from folklore. The instruction to remain still until music

The pavements outside Hereford's Kerry Arms are haunted by an inoffensive phantom

is heard, and then to flee, is usually linked to stories about fairies or other little people not well disposed toward humans. The overwhelming urge of an unwilling witness to go to meet the ghost is again a common feature of tales, as is the final line that the witness fell ill and died soon after. Such elements may be seen as embellishments added to an existing story to make it more exciting.

On the other side of the city, the Kerry Arms overlooks a stretch of pavement which is haunted by an old man. This old boy, often said to be 'Old Mr Hoskins', perhaps the same as the one seen around the cathedral, seems harmless enough, pottering about on business of his own and ignoring any passing humans.

Even more retiring is the ghostly Man in Black who might be encountered outside Mordiford. This impressive spectre takes the form of a tall man dressed in a long black overcoat or cloak, which he wears even on hot summer days. He walks with measured tread, but if anybody calls out to him or gets too close he simply vanishes into thin air.

The ghost at Madley haunts the B4352. He is rarely seen and although the locals firmly believe that he exists, and that he is linked somehow to a pot of gold coins found nearby some years ago, nobody seems entirely certain what he looks like.

The ghost that haunts the B4214 where it crosses the stream just north of the village of Staplow is quite different. She is well known both in appearance and story.

Back in the 18th century a mill stood by this road, grinding the local grains into flour to be used by the farmers or to be bagged up and sent off to market. The miller had a pretty and charming daughter who not unnaturally attracted the notice of the local young men, especially those who drove the carts to drop off grain or pick up flour.

The miller, however, had high hopes for his daughter. He knew her to be attractive, virtuous and intelligent, and hoped that she would marry well, improving his social standing and income in the process. He kept a watchful eye on young men callers to his mill. One day his

The lanes and fields around Mordiford are the haunt of a man in black

*The B4214 outside Staplow where it crosses
a small stream is haunted by a tragic ghost*

worst fears were justified when a tall, handsome but virtually penniless young farmboy approached him to ask for the daughter's hand in marriage.

The miller was furious, and cut the boy down in a fit of temper, then hurriedly disposed of the body. The flesh was fed to the miller's pigs and the bones thrown into the mill to be ground up and added to the next batch of flour.

The daughter, of course, knew that her beloved had been intending to visit her father. She was fobbed off with an invented story about how the young man had been offered a fine job many miles away and had left to seek his fortune.

For days afterward she was seen wandering disconsolately down by the stream, visiting the places where she had met her boyfriend away from the eyes of her father. Then one day she was found face down in the stream. Perhaps she had discovered the truth about her lover, or maybe she had simply given up hope of seeing him again. Whatever the precise cause of her death, her ghost returns to haunt the lane beside the stream. She wanders sadly, sometimes glancing up quickly as if looking for somebody who never comes.

Rather different is the ghost that can be heard, but not seen, on the hills north of Dorstone. Centuries ago the hills were home to a village, the inhabitants of which indulged in wickedness of many kinds — at least, so the old stories say. It is unfortunate that they do not record quite what the sins of this village were, as such details would have made the story easier to understand. But whatever the unnamed sins might have been, they were enough to call down the wrath of God. One afternoon an earthquake struck the area of the Golden Valley. A gaping chasm opened up in the hills and swallowed the sinful village whole. To this day the lanes north of Dorstone are haunted by a the sounds of a church bell tolling mournfully for the souls of the damned.

Disaster also overtook Pembridge many years ago. It seems that it was not an excess of wickedness that caused this cataclysm, but sheer bad luck. One evening a dance was to be held in Pembridge, which then stood rather to the

A spectral bell echoes over the hills north of Dorstone

north-east of its current location. A fiddler from Eardisland was engaged for the evening.

All went well and a merry old time was had by all. Eventually the dance ended and the fiddler set off to walk home to Eardisland. Just as he was reaching his front door he realised that he had left behind his white kid gloves, which were decorated with red ribbon. Rather annoyed, he turned around and walked back toward Pembridge.

He had almost reached the village when he turned a corner in the lane and stopped appalled. The entire settlement had gone, and where it had stood was spread a dismal, windswept marsh. The only survivors of the terrible inundation were those who had been away from home at the time, and it was they who built Pembridge where it now stands. The marshes beside the River Arrow have now been drained, but as at Dorstone the phantom sounds of long vanished church bells can be heard on quiet evenings.

Even more enigmatic is the ghostly 'something' that haunts the road to Hereford out of Hoarwithy. The haunted spot is on top of a hill where local suicides were traditionally buried. Presumably the ghost is the phantom of one of these unhappy souls, though it is impossible to be certain. The strange presence is, however, capable of terrifying horses, dogs and other animals and will cause them to bolt uncontrollably.

8 Nameless Phantoms

There are a good number of ghosts that have no name and not much by way of a story behind them. Rather annoyingly for the ghost hunter investigating hauntings and stories of the paranormal, these nameless phantoms very often turn out to be the most active ghosts about.

A particular class of haunting is known these days as a poltergeist, German for 'noisy ghost'. In years gone by these visitations were generally held to be due to a visiting member of the fairy race, or perhaps a junior demon — sometimes called a familiar. In 1670 such an event took place at Burton, as recorded in a contemporary letter written by a gentleman of Hereford to a friend:

> There is a farm in Burton, a village in the parish of Weobley, which Mr William Bridges, a linen draper of London, has in mortgage from one Thomas Tomkyns, a decayed yeoman. This farm was taken in lease of Mrs Elizabeth Bridges about Michaelmas 1669. Soon after this tenant was entered on the farm, some familiar began to act apish pranks by knocking boldly at the door in the dark of the evening, and the like early in the morning, but nobody to be seen. The stools and forms [wooden benches] were thrown into disorder, heaps of malt and vetches mingled, loaves of bread laid on a table carried into another room, or hid in tubs covered with cloths. Cabbage plants dug up and replanted in various patterns; a half roasted pig demolished except the bones; the milk turned sour with vinegar, some cattle died and among others a sow leaped and danced in strange postures and at last fell down dead; a mow of pulse and pease likewise.
>
> After these one John Jones, a valiant Welshman, undertook to keep watch with a sword, a mastiff dog and a lantern. He had not long lain on the bed when he heard a knocking at the door, and as he conceived many cats came into his chamber, broke the windows and made a hideous noise. The mastiff howled, the candle went out, the Welshman fell into a cold sweat, left the sword unused and with much

ado found the door and ran half a mile without looking behind him, protesting next day he would not be another night in the house for a hundred pounds. These particulars I received from eye witnesses of unquestionable credit and you may no more doubt the truth of them than distrust the affection of

    Your humble servant

    JA

The haunting of the Burton farmhouse caused quite a sensation at the time. From the description it would undoubtedly be classed by modern ghost hunters as the activities of a poltergeist.

Unlike most ghosts, poltergeists are never seen, but they do indulge in all sorts of physical tricks and pranks. A poltergeist visitation usually begins, as did that in 1669, with knocking or rapping noises which sound exactly as if a person was knocking with their knuckles on wood. At Burton these began on the door, but they might just as easily come from inside wardrobes, under beds or from empty rooms. The knockings will last for some weeks, even months. They may fade away and the haunting end, or they may increase in volume and frequency as the haunting moves up a notch.

From knocking, the poltergeist will often progress on to moving objects about. At Burton this involved moving bread, shifting furniture and mixing up harvested crops. The vast majority of poltergeists progress no further than such annoying, but essentially harmless pranks. They will continue for a few weeks, then cease and the haunting revert to knockings that become increasingly weak.

A few poltergeists, like that at Burton, become stronger still and more destructive. At Burton animals were killed and crops destroyed. Modern cases often involve clothes, beds or books being set on fire. This peak of destructive activity rarely lasts more than a few days before it fades back to mere pranks, and then to knocking.

A very few cases will involve a disembodied voice, or words written on walls, that usually convey hideous threats jumbled up with childish verse or incoherent ramblings.

Exactly what causes a poltergeist haunting is a matter of some dispute. The gentleman back in 1670 had no doubt that it was caused by a 'familiar'; others at the time would have blamed the fairies. More recently people tend to blame ghosts or disembodied spirits.

Investigators have noted a number of common factors that seem to link all poltergeist outbreaks and study those to try to establish a cause. The most obvious features of an attack concern the progression of events, as outlined above.

In addition there is almost always a person, rather than a place, at the centre of the haunting. If the person moves house, the poltergeist will move with them rather than remaining at the first house. This 'focus', as investigators term the person, is almost always a teenager, usually a girl, who is undergoing some sort of emotional stress.

Some think that the poltergeist activity is faked by the troubled teenager as a way of gaining attention. However, several investigations have taken precautions that rule this out. Assuming that the phenomena are genuinely paranormal, there are two theories that currently have their supporters.

The first considers that the troubled teenager is causing the poltergeist manifestations unconsciously and inadvertently. Some people claim to have telekinetic powers — that is, the ability to move objects without touching them and using the powers of thought alone. If these powers exist, and conventional science does not accept that they do, then an emotionally overwrought teenager may use them to lash out randomly in an effort to deal with the powerful feelings they experience.

Others believe that the emotional youngster attracts the attentions of a spiritual entity of some kind. The entity is able to break through to the human world by taking advantage of the tense atmosphere of the house. Once having made contact with the material world, the entity will then play practical jokes and tricks to amuse itself at the expense of the humans

It should be stated that conventional science does not accept that there is anything paranormal involved in poltergeist events. Scientists prefer either to ignore the phenomenon or to ascribe it to human trickery — though often without any evidence to back up the claim. The attitude seems to be that poltergeists cannot exist, so therefore they don't.

A more conventional spectre is the gentleman in the wide-brimmed hat who haunts Prior's Court at Callow. The fashions of the ghost seem to place him in the 17th century, while the flamboyant hat and jacket on which witnesses remark have encouraged many to state that he is a Cavalier. Tradition has it that he was walled up alive here during the Civil War and left to die by heartless Roundhead troopers. There is no documentary evidence that the story is true. However, it is known that Lord Leven and his Scottish army swept through here in July 1645. Leven's Scots acquired an ugly reputation for looting and violence, though whether even they would have been capable of such coldly ruthless treatment is not certain. With a few notorious exceptions, the Civil War was fought out according to the rules of war as they were generally accepted in the 17th century.

The unnamed hurdle maker of Longtown has a less bloody origin. He lived a blameless and worthy life quietly chopping and twisting hazel wands

A ghostly hurdlemaker haunts the fields and woods around Longtown Castle

into hurdles for the use of local shepherds. When he died, he was buried respectably enough, but was soon back as a ghost. He was seen and heard frequently in the copses and woods where hazel grew.

On the advice of a local wizard, or wise man, the villagers dug up the man's coffin and turned it over before reburying it, but the corpse-turning had no effect on the ghost. The man continued to be seen and the tap-tap-tapping of his tools echoed through the woods. A year or so later a travelling Baptist minister came to Longtown. In the course of his sermon the minister denounced superstition and in particular the belief in ghosts. His congregation looked up to the haunted woods that they knew so well and snorted their disapproval.

Not only nameless, but also unseen, is the ghost of the Lough Pool pub at Sellack. This ghost moves invisibly and silently about the pub, but leaves in its wake the strong and unmistakable scent of lavender. Presumably the phantom is that of a lady. She will sometimes move chairs around in the bar area at night, presumably so that they are in positions that she favours.

The Crown Inn at Lea is also haunted, though in rather more dramatic fashion and by two ghosts. The pub was formerly two different properties and although the downstairs has been knocked through to create a single property, the upstairs remain separate and can be accessed only by way of different staircases.

It is the western of the two upstairs flats that is haunted by a woman in a flowing gown. She is seen most often beside a fireplace in the front room, but sometimes appears on the stairs leading down to the bar. This ghost is extremely active and leaves behind her a rather uneasy feeling, as if something awful is about to happen.

The Crown Inn at Lea is home to two of the most active ghosts in the county

Perhaps it is no wonder that the rooms she frequents have been abandoned by the pub's landlady. She does not care for the ghost, nor for the odd atmosphere that it creates. The haunted room is not used, while the rest of the flat is given over to storage so that the haunted stairs do not need to be used very often.

Rather less troublesome is the phantom man who haunts the area of the bar that lies toward the rear of the pub and is used as a restaurant. This is the ghost of an elderly man who sits quietly on an equally spectral chair beside a window. Most of the time he just sits there gazing benevolently about, but the old boy seems to get quite irate when anything is placed where he likes to sit.

In 2005 a new member of staff was given the task of putting up

The ghostly lady of the Crown Inn frequents this upstairs chamber. It has been abandoned by the pub staff, largely on account of its ghostly resident

the Christmas decorations. Seeing an empty spot next to a window that she thought would make an ideal place for a Christmas tree, she set up the tree and went to work decorating it with a will. Job finished, she went off to make a cup of tea. She had taken only two steps into the kitchen when there was an almighty crash from the restaurant area. Hurriedly returning she saw the Christmas tree over-turned and all her carefully arranged baubles scattered over the floor. The landlady quickly put her right and advised her to place the tree elsewhere. She did, and no further mishaps occurred.

The second ghost at the Crown at Lea sits quietly in this room, beside the window to the right of the picture

Between them the two ghosts of the Crown put in an appearance about once a month, making them among the most often seen spectres of Herefordshire. Whether or not they are linked in any way, there is no way of knowing.

The Mount Craig Hotel at Pencraig is said to be haunted, but no reliable witnesses can be found to explain by whom, or how often the ghost is seen. A similarly vague spectre is said to haunt the Black Lion on Hereford's Bridge Street. He is said to be a man dressed in a green suit, but otherwise nothing is known of him. Another anonymous phantom is said to lurk in the Pengethley Manor Hotel near Ross on Wye. And yet another phantom — a lady — is reputed to walk the chambers of the Holme Lacy House Hotel, a converted 17th century manor house near Hereford.

The Kings Head Hotel in the High Street of Ross-on-Wye has a strong local reputation for being haunted. The 14th-century inn is certainly full of atmosphere, with its oak beams, ancient fireplaces and old paintings. The man in black who is said to haunt the place has not been seen in recent years, though one member of staff is adamant that there is 'something odd' about the place.

The Kings Head Hotel at Ross on Wye has a strong local reputation for being haunted

The ghost of the King Charles II Hotel in Ross on Wye's Broad Street has slightly more evidence to back it up. In 1973 a photo of the hotel showed the ghost peering out of the window of an empty room. In 2003 a *Hereford Times* photographer named James Watkins experienced problems when trying to copy the photo using a digital camera. No matter where he put the flash, it always reflected off the image of the ghost, ruining the copy. Then, in the one copy where the flash did not get in the way, an odd red blur obliterated the ghost instead.

The Talbot Hotel in Leominster's West Street is a warm and attractive old coaching inn. Before it was built, the crossroads near which it stands was known as the Iron Cross, and was where criminals were hanged. The most famous execution to take place on this spot was that of Roger Cadwallader, a Roman Catholic priest, in 1610.

It was in the early 17th century that religious disputes between Protestant and Catholic Christians were at their most bloody in England. Only five years earlier a conspiracy led by Robert Catesby had hired the infamous Catholic mercenary Guy Fawkes to blow up Parliament, and King James I with it. The plan had been to wipe out the Protestant king and bishops at a stroke, and so open the way for a Catholic rebellion. The plan misfired and the conspirators were executed.

There was a widespread suspicion, very often proved true, that Catholic agents from abroad were coming to England to stir up rebellion and to try to murder members of the government or the royal family. Of particular concern to the security services were British Catholics who had been abroad to attend schools or seminaries of the Catholic Church. Such people could blend inconspicuously with the local population while stirring up trouble and planning terrorist actions. As a result, attending a Catholic school abroad and returning to England without declaring the fact to the government was made a capital crime. The Catholics of England — most of whom were loyal to the kingdom, though they might object to the king's religion — protested that they needed Catholic priests to minister to their religious needs and conduct ceremonies.

At this distance in time it is impossible to be certain quite where Roger Cadwallader fitted into this dangerous religious milieu. He was arrested in Herefordshire in 1609 and brought before the assizes of 1610 in Leominster. (The trials had been moved from Hereford due to an outbreak of the plague.)

Cadwallader was a native of Stretton Sugwas, near Hereford, who came from a Catholic family. He had gone to Spain, then Italy to pursue his studies and had been ordained as a priest in the Catholic faith. He then returned to England to work as a travelling priest conducting religious rites for the Catholic families of the western counties. Whether or not he was engaged in stirring up rebellion or planning terrorist acts it is now impossible to say as the evidence has not been preserved. Beyond doubt, however, he returned to England secretly and so had broken the law.

He was duly found guilty by the court of having been ordained abroad and returning secretly, and, the penalty being death, he was hanged, and his head was put up on a spike over the Lugg Bridge. In 1988 he was beatified by Pope John Paul II to become the Blessed Roger Cadwallader, a step that put him on the road to sainthood.

Ever since it was built in the 17th century, the Talbot Hotel has been visited by a dark figure dressed in a long cloak and wearing a hood. He has been habitually identified as a monk, but it seems more likely that he is the phantom of Cadwallader come back to haunt the site of his execution.

Not far away is Croft Castle, a 14th century fortified manor house. The ghost here is tall and imposing. One witness who came face to face with him in the 1990s estimated him to be about seven feet tall.

More enigmatic still is the 'strange presence' that lurks at the manor house at Eardisland. Meanwhile, a spiritualist who visited Eastnor Castle declared it to contain no less than thirteen ghosts, though none of them could be identified with any certainty.

But perhaps the strangest haunting is that of the ancient megalithic tomb just north of Dorstone that is known as Arthur's Stone. Some people who visit the place report hearing a strange, low frequency buzzing sound that gradually increases in volume until it is almost deafening, when it abruptly ceases. No normal source of this noise has been ever been found.

9 Untimely Deaths

Whatever one's views on the causes of hauntings or the reality of ghosts, there can be no doubt that a number of the more active hauntings are linked to tragic deaths of one kind or another.

Some would hold that the massive emotional impact of the sad events have imprinted themselves on the surroundings and caused the hauntings Others might maintain that the often sudden and always untimely nature of the deaths have kept the spirits of those involved chained to this earth to walk as spectres. The more cynical would suggest that brutal events are the sort of thing that get remembered by local people and can give rise to stories of ghosts when no such things exist.

Whatever one's views, it must be admitted that the events that unfolded at Aconbury are typical of the type. Many years ago a young farmhand was in the habit of meeting his girlfriend in a patch of woodland overlooking the church. There they could meet away from the prying eyes of their neighbours to whisper sweet nothings and discuss their future together.

Gradually, however, the girl came to believe that her lover was being untrue. Exactly how she came to form this impression is not known, but once the green-eyed demon of jealousy had taken hold it came to consume her. Her boyfriend had only to talk to another woman after church for the girl to see it as evidence of his disloyalty. She confronted him with her suspicions, but his denials only served to confirm her views. After all, he would deny that he loved another, would he not? — especially if he were misleading the girl to keep her sweet.

She planned a bloody revenge. Taking an old shotgun from her father's farm she went to meet her lover in the woods. Again she demanded to know the truth, again he protested his innocence. Consumed by jealousy and anger she shot him dead. The gun blast brought villagers running, but the girl made no attempt to escape. She was suddenly overwhelmed by grief at what she had done. A second shot cut short her own life. By the time the villagers arrived, it was only to find two corpses.

The woods behind Aconbury church were the site of a tragic event that resulted in a haunting

Ever since that tragic double death the woods have been haunted by the lovers. They wander at peace with each other, obviously playing out happy memories of their early time together before the fatal jealousy took hold.

Another tragic death caused the haunting of the churchyard at Aylton. In 1856 the 14-year-old Emma Foulger was walking downstairs at her family home of Aylton Court as her elder brother came home from a hunting expedition. The young man tripped and fell, dropping his shotgun which went off. The shot struck the hapless Emma in the chest and she died within minutes.

The poor girl's body was carried to the tiny church at Aylton, where she was laid to rest by her grieving family, but she did not rest in peace for long. Two days after the funeral a passerby noticed something odd in the churchyard. He walked over and was horrified to see that the grave had been dug up and the body stolen.

It was assumed at the time that the body had been stolen by what were known as 'resurrectionists'. These macabre villains dug up freshly buried corpses and took them off to the large cities where they would sell them for cash to the less scrupulous of the doctors who were teaching anatomy. At this date it was illegal to use human bodies to teach anatomy unless they were those of executed criminals or suicides whose families had given permission. Perhaps it was thought that poor Emma's injuries could be passed off as those of a suicide, particularly to a doctor who did not ask too many questions.

The Foulger family sent out agonised appeals to the medical schools begging for the return of their daughter's body should it be offered for sale, but the body was never tracked down. Perhaps it had already been cut up by some heartless doctor who was then afraid to confess that he had done so.

Whatever happened to the body, the ghost walks at the churchyard still. The ghost of young Emma wanders about apparently quite happily. She seems to pick flowers, skip about and appears to be generally enjoying herself in an innocent girlish way — at least according to those who have seen her.

Altogether darker are the two ghosts of Much Dewchurch. Back in 1861, Charles Bodenham of Much Dewchurch was locked in a deep dispute with Robert Pye

The little church at Aylton is one of the most charming in Herefordshire, but it holds an old tragedy

of the Mynde. The argument was over land rights and was so complex and deep that it had already taken up a fair degree of court time. Both men seem to have been obstinate types, for neither would back down and neither would even contemplate a compromise.

The dispute was made worse by the fact that the two men had already been engaged in a religious argument of some fervour. Pye was an ardent Protestant, while Bodenham was a Catholic of equal enthusiasm. This was a religious age when differences of theology were taken very seriously.

As part of the grinding legal process, Pye obtained a court summons against Bodenham and set out to serve it on him. He caught up with his neighbour outside the church at Much Dewchurch. Realising what was happening, Bodenham fled, but Pye caught up with him. The confrontation occurred in the shade of a walnut tree to the east of the church, but most of that area has since been built on, and the precise spot cannot now be identified.

Pye tried to thrust the court summons into Bodenham's hands, but the man fought back and in the scuffle that followed, Pye was stabbed through the heart, and died. There was never much doubt as to Bodenham's guilt, but the case excited enormous interest both because the land case was well known and because Bodenham had no reputation for violence. He was hanged, all the same.

The ghosts of the pair were seen many times in the years that followed the killing, fleeing from the church, then fighting under the walnut tree. Sadly for ghost hunters, they do not seem to have appeared recently.

Another murder victim may be seen in spectral form around Weobley, near to Dunwood Farm. The unfortunate victim was Old Gregg, an elderly farmer who had for some reason incurred the enmity of his own son. The younger man slipped a stewed toad into his father's supper and so consigned him a painful and lingering death. The reason for the killing was never discovered for the younger Gregg never explained his actions.

Old Gregg appears in country clothes of a bygone age: smock, wide-brimmed hat and boots. He walks around what were once his acres peacefully enough.

It was an accidental death that led to the haunting of a shop in Hereford's High Street. The building dates back to the 17th century, but the death occurred in the 18th century. The shop was then home to an apothecary — a chemist we would call him these days. As was the custom then, the apothecary bought in a wide variety of chemicals, herbs, plant extracts and the like. He then made them up into a variety of preparations on the premises. Some of these were widely known, while others were of his own invention. He would make up medicines for humans, horses and plants. He might produce fly papers and pesticides, make up and skin cleansers, dyes and preservatives — anything, in fact, that a busy rural city might need in the way of chemicals.

This was in the days before the law required such men to keep a 'poisons book', a ledger in which was recorded all poisonous substances that the apothecary bought, what he made them into and to whom they were sold. Back then only a limited number of deadly chemicals were available, so they had to be used for many purposes. Preparations to kill weeds were as likely to kill humans, as were fly-papers and even some cosmetics, if they were ingested in quantity. And some people deliberately ate small quantities of arsenic for the drug-like high that it gave them.

It was therefore incumbent on the apothecary to keep a careful note of what chemicals he put in what product, and in what quantity. But one day he made a terrible error. Some powders got mixed up, or put in the wrong jars. Whatever the cause, deadly poison was put into some pills by mistake. The apothecary's assistant took one and dropped dead. The apothecary never recovered from the accident. He fell into a fit of depression and died soon after. His ghost returns to the scene to wander about muttering endlessly of his remorse.

The background to the ghost of the Boot Inn at Orleton is less clear-cut, though the haunting is clear enough. It takes the form of a piano in

The ghost at Orleton's Boot Inn was most active in the 1990s

the bar playing what seems to be a rather stately dance tune. The music usually comes at night and is sometimes accompanied by the sounds of doors opening and closing and of footsteps trotting back and forth across the bar.

There are, however, different versions of what lies behind the haunting. One version has it that it was caused by a bitter feud between a former landlord of the pub and the man who had been his senior member of staff. The dispute may have been over some money that had gone missing from the till, but whatever started it off the ill feeling grew to be very deep.

Some say that the landlord painted his former friend out of a picture, others that the two came to blows. Either way the barman died suddenly, apparently of natural causes. The haunting began soon after and continues to the this day. The phantom piano was especially active in the 1990s.

Another haunted pub is the New Inn at Pembridge. This is the epitome of what a rural pub in Herefordshire should be like. It has a striking black-and-white timbered exterior, a flagstone floor and oak doors with wooden latches. The building began life as a farmhouse in 1311 and later served as a local courthouse and meeting hall. Although it has been much altered since, bits of the original structure still stand. The name of 'New Inn' refers to the fact that the building became a pub fairly recently, not to the age of the building. Indeed the place likes to boast that it is the oldest New Inn in England.

The New Inn has two ghosts. They never appear together, but there is reason to believe that the two are linked. The upstairs ghost is that of a young woman in a long gown, said to have been the daughter of the farmer who lived here in years gone by. Her lover went off to seek fame and fortune

The ancient New Inn at Pembridge has two ghosts, though they never seem to meet.
The rear bar (below) is the room where the ghostly soldier is seen most often

in the wars, but found only a cold grave. The poor woman died of a broken heart when she heard the news. Interestingly, she appears only to women.

The second ghost is seen only downstairs. He is a soldier dressed in a red tunic, such as British soldiers wore in the days before improved weaponry made camouflage necessary. He is sometimes seen carrying a sword, and at other times banging soundlessly on a side drum. Whether this is the missing soldier so eagerly awaited by the lady upstairs there is no way of knowing.

Perhaps one day they will meet and all will be well.

11 The Devil Came Calling

The Devil is a lively character in stories of the supernatural that are found in Herefordshire. Indeed, it is noticeable that the evil one is mentioned far more often in Herefordshire than in most English counties. Why this should be so tends to divide people. Those from outside the county are apt to remark that Satan will find his work easier to do in Herefordshire. Those who live here reply that he has to spend more time in the county for precisely the opposite reason — that Herefordshire folk are less likely to sin and so he needs to put in extra effort.

The figure of the Devil is, of course, drawn from the Bible. The name means 'accuser' in Greek and is thought to refer to the fact that the role of the Devil was to tempt humans to sin so that he could collect evidence with which to accuse them on the Day of Judgement. His other name in the Bible, Satan, is the same word in Hebrew.

Since the Bible was written a whole and hugely complex mythology has grown up about the Devil and his minions. Some of this is sanctioned by some Christian denominations, but much of it is entirely unofficial and has no grounding in theology. The Devil is generally thought to be hugely powerful, but to have no hold over humans or their souls unless the person involved willingly agrees to this. The idea of selling your soul to the Devil in return for worldly power or wealth is an old one. The Devil is widely held to be utterly ruthless and deeply cunning when agreeing to such pacts. He is skilled at twisting words to his meaning and so cheating the human, but he is also likely to make mistakes and to be cheated in his turn.

The Devil is also believed to be able to take on human form. In earlier times he would usually appear as a rich and successful stranger, mounted on a fine horse — these days presumably he would drive a Rolls Royce or a Ferrari — and be dressed in the costliest fashions. There is usually something wrong about this disguise that can be detected by the more astute, though sometimes not until it is too late. He may, for instance, leave his feet as cloven hooves.

Nor does the Devil come alone. He has demons and minions to do his bidding. Some of these have names — Beelzebub and Astaroth are among the better known — but others are nameless. These demons are usually thought of as being less powerful than their evil master, but still to be deeply dangerous.

Whatever the truth, it is certain that the Devil features strongly in Herefordshire tales. Some of these seem to be folktales with little, if any, basis in fact. Others are rooted in truth and use the Devil as a personification of evil to explain events. Still more seem to be authentic tales about seemingly supernatural happenings, except that those involved ascribe the events to the Devil rather than to ghosts or spectres.

Take, for instance, the story of how the Devil and his wife came to the rectory at Grosmont some two centuries or so ago. The story has been overlain with various layers and added to over the years, but in essence it seems to be about a poltergeist attack. There were the normal knockings and rappings by invisible hands on doors and wood panelling. Furniture was moved about the house, while small objects appeared and disappeared with baffling regularity.

This had been going on for some weeks when a pair of sailors passing through Grosmont approached the vicar with a proposition. They were, the two men said, widely travelled and experienced in all manner of strange and mysterious things. They undertook to rid the house of the supernatural trouble, if they were allowed to stay alone there overnight. They would need, the sailors said, £5 in payment — then the equivalent of about two months wages — plus a roast goose for supper and all the cider they could drink.

At his wits' end, the vicar agreed. The goose was set in the oven to roast, a barrel of cider in the cellar was broached and the money was paid over. The two sailors took up residence. Next day the vicar and his family returned to find them slumped senseless in the kitchen, the kitchen window smashed and the furniture scattered and overturned. When the sailors woke up they told the following story.

They explored the house to rule out any trickery, then settled in the kitchen. About 10 o'clock, the goose being ready to eat, one of the sailors went down to the cellar to get some cider. Sitting on the barrel was none other than the Devil himself, grinning wickedly. The sailor fainted. The second sailor, wondering where his drink was, went down to find his friend. He too saw the Devil, but instead of fainting he boldly approached, saying loudly, 'By your leave, a jug of cider I must have.' He then drew off a jug of cider while the Devil watched. Then the sailor carried the jug and dragged his friend back to the kitchen.

The first sailor recovered his senses in time to start carving the goose while his companion refilled the depleted cider mugs. There was then a terrific crashing and banging from the chimney. Down came a terrible figure — it was the Devil's wife. She spied the roast goose and called out down the cellar steps, 'Mr Longtooth, Mr Longtooth. The goose is done.'

The bold sailor stood up at once and shouted at her, 'Done or not done, there's no goose for you.' The Devil's wife eyed him angrily, then climbed back up the chimney and was gone.

The meal eaten, the cider drunk, the two sailors went upstairs to bed. They had no sooner nodded off than they were awoken by a terrific noise from downstairs. The bold sailor leapt up and rushed down to find the Devil and his wife playing football around the house. They were scattering furniture left and right as they played. The sailor dived into the game and soon managed to get possession of the ball. 'Two to one is not fair', he cried out. 'And here is one for my landlord.' With that he kicked the ball as hard as he could at the kitchen window. The ball smashed through the glass and vanished into the night, quickly followed by the Devil and his wife.

The two sailors had then sat down in the kitchen, refilled the cider jug and bravely stayed on watch in case the Devil should return. He did not and so, the sailors concluded their story, the haunting was over.

Now it might be thought that the passing sailors, hearing the story of the haunting, had thought that they might get a free bed for the night, plus a roast goose and copious quantities of cider by offering to help. It might also be thought that they drank themselves senseless on the vicar's cider, then invented the story about the Devil and his wife to explain the mess and to be able to claim success.

All of that might be true, of course, but it is a fact that the haunting ceased abruptly. Poltergeists are discussed more fully in the chapter on Nameless Phantoms, but what is interesting about this case is that the sailors told their story with great conviction and were obviously believed by those to whom they were talking. As noted in that chapter, some researchers think that poltergeists are caused inadvertently by emotionally troubled people who seek a release though telekinetics. In this case it might be that the person unconsciously causing the haunting believed that the sailors had indeed driven out the Devil and that the haunting was over. Believing it was over, made it so.

Another instance where the Devil was blamed for something different comes from the medieval chronicle of Bartholomew de Cotton. In 1290 he wrote that:

An unheard of and almost impossible marvel occurred in the Cathedral Church of the Hereford Canons. There a demon in the robes of a canon sat in a stall after matins had been sung. A canon came up to him and asked his reason for sitting there, thinking that the demon was a brother canon. The latter refused to answer and said nothing. The canon was terrified, but believing the demon to be an evil spirit put his trust in the Lord and bade him in the name of Christ and St Thomas de Cantilupe not to stir from that place. For a short time he bravely awaited speech. Receiving no answer he at last went for help. He beat the demon and put him in fetters. He now lies in the prison of the aforesaid St Thomas de Cantilupe.

It is difficult to know what to make of this demonic appearance. It seems unlikely that any demon would allow itself to be beaten and chained by a monk, though it may be that the canons of Hereford were particularly skilled when it came to overcoming evil. A modern, rational mind might think that the 'demon' was some poor human suffering from mental illness who behaved in such a fashion as to convince the canon that he was a demon — perhaps he failed to show proper respect to a cross or the statue of a saint. If so, it must be hoped that he was recognised for what he was before the canons did him any real harm.

Another demon has taken up more or less permanent residence on the Black Mountains west of Longtown. This demon likes nothing better than to tempt travellers to their doom. His favourite trick is to blow out lanterns on even the stillest night. Thus plunged into darkness, travellers may well stumble into difficulties. If they were to fall and break a bone, they would be lucky not to succumb to exposure on the wild slopes, especially during winter. Those who have seen the Longtown Demon report that it is small and black with wings and a harsh cry.

It was not some mere underling demon that came to Shobdon, but the Devil himself. The evil one had been roused to anger by the beautiful church that the people of the village had built to the glory of God. Grabbing his mighty shovel, the Devil heaved up a vast amount of earth and set off to dump it on the church of Shobdon. As he strode toward the village he met a cobbler heading the other way, towards Kington. Seeing the Devil coming, the cobbler was so frightened that he dropped the sack of shoes that he had collected to be mended.

'Is this Shobdon?' demanded the Devil in his awful voice. The cobbler was fortunately sharp-witted and recovered quickly from his shock. 'Why, no', he replied. 'I'm looking for it myself, and I've worn out all these shoes on the road. I can't find it anywhere round here. You'd better turn back.'

Cursing volubly the Devil dropped his shovelful of earth and stomped off back to Hell. The mound of earth he created can still be seen. The story is spoiled only by the fact that an archaeological dig has revealed the mound to be a prehistoric burial mound created by human hands.

Another prehistoric monument to have demonic links is the megalithic stone that stands at Colwall. It is said that at midnight, when a full moon shines down on the village, the Devil will appear beside the stone. Grasping it in his powerful talons, the Devil turns the stone around, then he vanishes. It is presumed that this story dates back to the earliest days of Christianity in Herefordshire when such obvious reminders of the pagan religion as the standing stone of Colwall were demonised.

The Devil also likes to visit the Stanner Rocks, an outcrop of boulders near Kington. There he stands to survey Herefordshire and keep a careful watch for those up to no good. While there he takes the time to tend his little garden — tearing out any living thing that grows to leave the ground barren and bare, just as he likes it.

The Devil is also a regular visitor to Dorstone. Every year at midnight on Hallowcen, the Devil appears in the churchyard dressed as a monk. He then makes his way into the church which is lit up by unearthly candles. The Devil climbs into the pulpit to preach a sermon of pure evil to the souls of those buried in the churchyard over the previous year whose sins have marked them down for Hell. He goes on to name those who are to die in the forthcoming year and are likewise doomed.

It is said that back in the early 19th century a local young man of famously drunken habits was stumbling back home past the church one Halloween when he saw lights appearing. Made bold by his intake of cider, the young

Once each year the Devil comes to Dorstone church to preach a sermon of evil

man wandered through the churchyard to have a look. Peering through a window he saw the Devil in the pulpit, and the first words he heard spoken were his own name.

Hurrying home, the young man collapsed and woke up the next day a changed man. He stopped drinking, attended church regularly and got his affairs in order. When he died a short time later, he did so with a clear conscience and so cheated the Devil of his soul.

The Devil was rather more successful at Kingsland. About 600 years ago the good folk of that parish needed a new church. They hired the stonemasons and bought the stone, and work began. Next day when the workers arrived on site all their work had been undone. This happened for several days, after which a local wizard, or wise man, was consulted. He assured the villagers that the Devil objected to the site of the church near Lawton, and advised them to choose another site. This they did, which is why the church stands where it does.

In fact, the reason why the church of Kingsland parish stands where it does is because the medieval lords of the manor insisted that it should be built close to the castle. That castle has long since gone —

The church at Kingsland was built on its present site after the Devil made his views known

only a few mounds of earth show where it once stood — so the church does seem to be in an inconvenient place. Maybe the tale recalls some dispute between the villagers and their lord about the site of the church.

As if the Devil does not come calling in Herefordshire often enough, there are places where he can be summoned. One of these is Tarrington. All that is needed is for a person to walk backwards around the church seven times while reciting the Lord's Prayer in reverse. If he then hurries to the church door and peeps in, he will see the Devil himself. The same ritual will also summon up the evil one at Stoke Edith church.

The task is rather easier at Weobley. Rather than walk all the way around the entire church, it is necessary only to walk around the large cross in the churchyard, but still reciting the Lord's Prayer backwards. The Devil will then appear, ready to seal any bargain that the person who raised him should want.

The most famous stories about the Devil in Herefordshire all relate to a mysterious and powerful medieval wizard by the name of Jack of Kent. This

The churchyard cross at Weobley. The Devil may be summoned here with some ease, though he may not prove so easy to get rid of

master magician did not come from Kent, but from the Herefordshire village of Kentchurch. He was famous as early as 1595, when he pops up as a minor character in a play by Anthony Munday, though it is clear from the play that he was thought to have lived a century or so earlier.

Scholars have argued at some length over who Jack of Kent might have been in reality, for there does seem to have been some real personage lurking behind the many stories that are told of him. John Kent, for instance, was vicar of Kentchurch in the 1520s, whilst another John Kent was a 15th century astrologer. John Gwent was a Welsh scholar who died in Hereford in 1348. There are other candidates, but none of them closely fit the few things that are known about Jack of Kent — that he was born into a humble family of farm labourers and that he lived most of his adult life at Kentchurch. That is all that is known for certain about the man; beyond that legend takes over.

The most usual version of Jack of Kent's life is that when he was still a boy he sold his soul to the Devil. In return he was given a personal demon who would do his bidding for as long as he lived. When Jack died the demon would carry his soul off to Hell, whether he was buried inside the church or outside it. This imp was no bigger than a fly and was kept inside a short black stick that Jack carried tucked inside his coat.

Jack's powers first came to the notice of his neighbours when he was about nine years old. The farmer for whom he worked gave him the task of guarding the newly sown fields of grain against the crows, but Jack wanted to go to Hereford Fair with his friends. The farmer soon realised that the boy had absconded, and as evening came he went to wait by the road from Hereford intent on giving him a sound beating. When Jack arrived he grinned at the farmer and said 'Don't ye worry. The crows be all right. They be all in the barn.' And so they were, sitting in neat rows waiting for sunset when the spell cast by Jack ended and they could fly free.

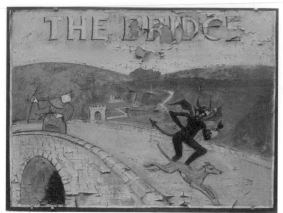

The rather battered pub sign of the Bridge Inn at Kentchurch depicts one of the most famous stories about the Devil in Herefordshire

Among Jack's wonders was a spare suit of clothes that could do the work of ten men. If grain needed threshing or straw baling, Jack would set his suit of clothes to do the work while he himself played on his fiddle.

Jack was also able to summon up the Devil to work for him. On one occasion he asked him to build a bridge over the River Monnow. The Devil agreed, but asked for the soul of the first person to cross the new bridge. Jack agreed, and the Devil built the bridge in a single night. At dawn the Devil stood by waiting to claim his payment, but Jack was too quick for him. Before any humans could approach, he threw a loaf of bread over the bridge and a dog scampered after it, so the Devil got only a dog for his pains.

One year, Jack of Kent got the Devil to plough all the fields around Kentchurch. Jack went around sowing the seeds then asked the Devil if he wanted the top of the crop or the bottom in payment. The Devil said the bottom. But Jack had tricked him by sowing gravel, not seed. He then went out and sowed grain. The Devil got the straw, while Jack got the grain.

Next year, Jack again got the Devil to plough the land. The Devil was not to be caught out twice, so this year he checked that Jack really was sowing seeds. Then the Devil said he would have the tops of the crop. But Jack had tricked him again by planting turnips, so the Devil got only leaves.

The stories are many and they always emphasise Jack's great powers and cunning, and how he always outwitted the Devil. His greatest trick, however, came after he was dead.

Jack left very precise instructions about his funeral. Most important of all was the stipulation that he must be buried in a cavity hollowed out of the wall of Kentchurch church. When the little black demon came to take his soul, he found that Jack had been buried neither inside nor outside the church and so his soul was not forfeit to the Devil.

If you should chance to be near Kentchurch you should take the time to visit the church. Go inside and you will see a fine medieval painting of Jack of Kent on the wall, marking the site of his unusual burial.

Index